Harry Hoppe

LAUREL & HARDY
LIFE & MAGIC

deutsch/english

Trescher Verlag

Trescher Verlag
Reinhardtstraße 9
D-10117 Berlin-Mitte
Tel.: +49(0)30 / 283 24 96
Fax: +49(0)30 / 281 59 94

© Trescher Verlag, 2001
2. Auflage 2001

Gewidmet / Dedicated to
Andreas Meier

Fotos / Photos
Laurel & Hardy Archiv, Hoppe
Archivkatalog, Hoppe

Lektorin / Lecturer
Sabine Herbener
Englische Übersetzung / Translation
Nigel J. Luhman

Umschlaggestaltung / Cover
Volker Oeljeklaus, Berlin
Layout / Design
Rotation Verlag-Service, Berlin
Sybille Zerling

Druck / Printing
Druckhaus Berlin Centrum

Printed in Germany
ISBN 3-928409-27-1

Die Deutsche Bibliothek — CIP-Einheitsaufnahme
Laurel & Hardy : life & magic ; ein
biographischer Filmband / Hoppe, Harry. - 1. Aufl. - Berlin :
(Trescher-Reihe Kultur)
ISBN 3—928409—27—1
NE: Hoppe, Harry; Laurel and Hardy; Laurel und Hardy

Stan Laurel   Oliver Hardy

(16.06.1890 – 23.02.1965)   (18. 01.1892 – 07. 08.1957)

Inhaltsverzeichnis

Table of contents

Vorwort

Von vielen wird Charlie Chaplin als „König der Komiker" bezeichnet. Ohne Chaplins Werk abwerten zu wollen: Nimmt man die beim Publikum erzeugten Lacher als Bewertungsmaßstab, handelt es sich zweifellos bei Laurel und Hardy um die wahren, ungekrönten Häupter des Lachens - eines Lachens, das dem Betrachter ohne jeglichen „Sozialkitsch" oder Hintergedanken entlockt wird. Nie wollten Laurel und Hardy mit ihren Filmen die Welt verbessern oder mit erhobenem Zeigefinger auf soziale Mißstände hinweisen; ihnen ging es lediglich darum, das Zwerchfell ihres Publikums zu reizen. Viele Kritiker haben sich bis heute nicht damit abfinden können, daß Stan und Ollie stets „nur" komisch sein wollten und waren. Stattdessen versuchen viele von ihnen immer noch, tiefschürfende Bedeutungsmuster in die einzelnen Filme hineinzuinterpretieren. So hätte mancher Autor es besser beim Zusammentragen biographischer Fakten bewenden lassen sollen, anstatt zu versuchen, Stan und Ollies Filme bis ins kleinste Detail zu analysieren.

Da ich mich in erster Linie mehr als Sammler denn als Autor begreife, habe ich mich bemüht, den Text im vorliegenden Buch so knapp wie möglich zu halten und dabei auf persönliche Wertungen oder Analysen weitestgehend zu verzichten (für detailliertere Informationen empfehle ich Interessenten das im gleichen Verlag erschienene Buch über Laurel und Hardy von Christian Blees). Ziel des Buches ist es, beim Betrachter dieses „Fotoalbums" möglichst viele schöne Kindheits- und Kinoerinnerungen zu wecken.

Ohne die Hilfe und den guten Zuspruch vieler netter Menschen wäre dieses Buch in der vorliegenden Form nicht möglich gewesen. Danken möchte ich vor allem Christian Blees, der mir trotz Zeitmangels immer wieder beratend zur Verfügung stand. Ein spezieller Dank gilt auch Sabine Herbener und Sybille Zerling für zahlreiche stilistische und gestalterische Anregungen sowie Siep, Nicky und Marianne Bousma für einzelne Fotos, die in meiner Sammlung noch fehlten. Außerdem natürlich auch dem Trescher Verlag, der mir meinen langgehegten Traum vom eigenen Buch erfüllt - vor allem aber Stan und Ollie für viele vergnügliche Stunden.

Harry Hoppe

Foreword

Many people have called Charlie Chaplin the „King of Comedy". Without wishing to detract from Chaplin's work, if we take the audience's laughter as the yardstick, then without doubt Laurel and Hardy are the true uncrowned kings of laughter. A laughter which is evoked in the viewer without any kind of social message or ulterior motive. Laurel and Hardy never intended to change the world with their films nor wag their fingers at social injustices. Their only aim was to tickle their audiences. Many critics have been unable to come to terms with the fact that Stan and Ollie „only" wanted to be, and indeed were, funny. Instead, many of them are still trying to read profound interpretations into the individual films. Many a writer would have done better gathering biographical facts rather than trying to analyse Stan and Ollie's films down to the very last detail.

As I consider myself more a collector than an author, in this book I have tried to keep the texts as short as possible and to refrain from making subjective evalu-ations or analyses. (For more detailed information I would recommend Christian Blees's book on Laurel and Hardy, also published by Trescher.) The aim of this book is to remind the reader looking at this „photo album" of as many wonderful childhood and screen moments as possible.

This book would never have appeared in its present form without many people's kind assistance and encouragement. Above all, I would like to thank Christian Blees for always somehow finding the time to give me his advice. Special thanks are due to Sabine Herbener and Sybille Zerling for numerous stylistic corrections as well as to Siep, Nicky and Marianne Bousma for photos which were missing from my collection. And of course thanks to Trescher Verlag for fulfilling my long-cherished dream of writing my own book. But above all thanks to Stan and Ollie for many enjoyable hours.

Harry Hoppe

Jugend und Solokarriere

Youth and solo career

Stan Laurel wurde am 16. Juni 1890 in dem kleinen nordenglischen Ort Ulverston geboren. Es war eine komplizierte Geburt, und da seine gläubigen Eltern dachten, er würde nicht lange überleben, ließen sie ihn noch am selben Tag auf den Namen Athur Stanley Jefferson taufen. Den Nachnamen Laurel nahm er erst später, mit Beginn seiner Filmkarriere, an.

Die Eltern waren beide im Theatergeschäft tätig. Vater Arthur Jefferson war zunächst Schauspieler, machte sich jedoch später als Manager zahlreicher nordenglischer Theater einen Namen. Er arbeitete als Produzent und Regisseur und schrieb auch selbst dramatische Bühnenstücke, in denen seine Frau, Madge Metcalfe, häufig die Hauptrolle übernahm. Madge Metcalfe war eigentlich Sängerin, doch seit ihrer Heirat mit Arthur im Jahre 1884 fühlte sie sich zur Schauspielerei hingezogen. Ihre Paraderolle war das Darstellen sogenannter Vamps - ein Frauentyp, den die Schauspielerin Theda Bara Jahre später in vielen Stummfilmen perfekt verkörpern sollte.

Stan wuchs zunächst nicht mit Theaterluft auf. Da er in den ersten Jahren ein kränkliches Kind blieb, war er der einzige Sproß seiner Eltern, der bei seinen Großeltern in Ulverston aufwuchs. Das Haus Nummer 3 in der Argyle Street, in dem er geboren wurde, steht übrigens heute noch, und in Ulverston gibt es auch ein Laurel & Hardy Museum, welches ganzjährig geöffnet ist. Seine Geschwister, der ältere Bruder Gordon, die Schwester Beatrice Olga und sein jüngerer Bruder Edward, führten mit ihren Eltern ein Nomadenleben quer durch die Bühnen und Städte Nordenglands.

Ab seinem sechsten Lebensjahr lebte Stan dann bei seiner Familie. Von der Theaterwelt war er sogleich derart fasziniert, daß er seinen ersten eigenen Bühnenauftritt bereits mit 9 Jahren absolvierte, als er auf der Bühne in einem Stück des Vaters in ein Horn blasen durfte.

Stan Laurel was born on 16 June 1890 in the small town of Ulverston in the north of England. It was a complicated birth and since his religious parents thought he would not live long, they christened him the same day Arthur Stanley Jefferson. He adopted the surname Laurel later, at the start of his film career.

Both his parents worked in theatre. His father Arthur Jefferson was originally an actor but went on to make a name for himself as the manager of several northern English theatres. He worked as a producer and director and also wrote his own plays in which his wife, Madge Metcalfe, played the lead. Madge Metcalfe was really a singer but since being married to Arthur in 1884 she felt drawn towards acting. Her showpiece was playing vamps, the type of woman the actress Theda Bara was to capture perfectly years later.

Stan first did not grow up in the world of theatre. But since he started life as a sickly child, he was the only child who grew up at his grandparents' in Ulverston. (The house at no. 3 Argyle Street where he was born still stands today and in Ulverston there is also a Laurel and Hardy museum, open all year round.) His siblings, his elder brother Gordon, his sister Beatrice Olga and his younger brother Edward led the life of a nomad with their parents around the theatres and towns in the north of England.

From the age of six onwards Stan lived with his family. From the very start, he was so fascinated by the world of theatre that he made his first stage appearance at the age of nine, when he was allowed to blow a horn in one of his father's plays.

Stan was captivated by the stage and he loved appearing in front of an audience. Thus he persuaded his father to

Stan war von der Bühne begeistert, und es machte ihm Riesenspaß, vor Publikum aufzutreten. So drängte er den Vater, auf dem Dachboden des Elternhauses in Bishop Auckland eine Art Kindertheater einrichten zu dürfen. „A. J.", wie Arthur genannt wurde, ließ sich nicht lumpen und beauftragte ein paar seiner Bühnenarbeiter, Stan ein komplettes Theater mit Bühne, Beleuchtung und Sitzplätzen auf dem Speicher einzurichten. Er freute sich, daß sein Sohn so vom Theater begeistert war und sah in ihm schon den eigenen Nachfolger. Der kleine Stan gründete die „Arthur Jefferson Dramatic Society" und fungierte zugleich als Manager, Hauptdarsteller und Stückeschreiber. Wie sein Vater führte er nicht etwa Komödien, sondern Dramen auf. Mitspieler und Zuschauer setzten sich aus befreundeten Nachbarskindern zusammen; waren nicht alle der zirka 20 Sitzplätze besetzt, wurde auf der Straße nach weiteren „Opfern" gesucht. Doch da dramatische Stücke, von Kindern gespielt, auf unfreiwillige Art doch eher lustig wirken, merkte Stan schon bald, daß ihm das komödiantische Fach mehr lag als das ernste. In der Schule wurde er schnell zum Klassenclown, doch anders als bei den meisten dieser Sorte fand er in seinem Klassenlehrer nicht etwa einen Gegner seines komischen Auftretens, sondern einen begeisterten Anhänger. Jener Mr. Bates war vor allem von Stans Parodien anderer Lehrer begeistert, und so mußte Stan des öfteren nicht zur Strafe, sondern zur Belustigung des Lehrerkollegiums nachsitzen ... Seine schulischen Pflichtleistungen waren eher mittelmäßig, gab es doch zu Hause und im Theater immer lustigere Sachen als ausgerechnet Hausaufgaben zu machen. Da ihn Arthur eher als Nachfolger im Management denn auf der Bühne sehen wollte, steckte er ihn - sehr zu Stans Leidwesen - in ein Internat. Als das Dachbodentheater etwa ein Jahr später wegen einer umgestoßenen Petroleumlampe den Flammen zum Opfer fiel, war Stans „Bühnenkarriere" denn auch zunächst einmal beendet.

Um die Jahrhundertwende zogen die Jeffersons nach Glasgow, wo „A. J." den Managerposten des örtlichen Metropole Theatre übernahm. Stan besuchte wieder eine normale Schule und zog es vor, während des Unterrichts an seine Freizeit im Metropole zu denken, statt auf die Fragen der Lehrer zu antworten. Sein Vater schickte ihn nochmals auf eine andere Schule, wo er im Jahre 1906 seine schulische Laufbahn hinter sich brachte. Der Vater war nicht allzu besorgt, sah er doch in dem schon 16jährigen Sohn nach wie vor seinen Nachfolger als Manager, den er zunächst zu seinem Assistenten machen wollte. Stan war jedoch nicht so sehr an organisatorischen Aufgaben im Theater interessiert, sondern wollte nur noch eines werden: Komiker. Sein großes Vorbild war der seinerzeit berühmte englische Komiker Dan Leno. Doch Stan sah sich auch viele andere Komiker an und stellte sich aus deren besten Sketchen ein „eigenes" Bühnenprogramm zusammen. Die Uraufführung fand nicht etwa auf der Bühne seines Vaters statt, sondern auf Albert E. Pickards Kleinkunstbühne „Penny Arcade". Pickard war ein guter Freund

let him set up a kind of children's theatre in the attic of the family home in Bishop Auckland. A.J., as Arthur was called, did not scrimp and got some of his stagehands to build Stan a complete theatre with a stage, lighting and seating. He was pleased to see his son so taken with theatre and hoped he would follow in his father's footsteps. The young Stan founded the „Arthur Jefferson Dramatic Society" and was manager, leading actor and playwright all in one. Like his father, he not only produced comedies, but also drama too. Actors and audience were recruited from among the neighbours' children and if some of the 20 or so seats were still vacant, more „victims" were sought out on the street. Yet since drama played by children has more of an undesirable comic effect, Stan soon realised that comedy was more his genre than drama. At school, he soon became the classroom fool, but, in contrast to most stories of this type, his teacher was not adverse to his comic acting but instead was an enthusiastic fan! This Mr. Bates was mainly taken by Stan's mimicry of the other teachers, meaning that Stan often had to stay behind, not as punishment but to entertain the staffroom. His schoolwork was rather mediocre, since at home and in the theatre there were always more funny things to do than homework. Since Arthur viewed Stan as more of a successor in management than on stage, he sent him to a boarding school - much to Stan's dismay. When the attic theatre was destroyed by fire around a year later due to an overturned paraffin lamp, it meant the end of Stan's „stage career" for the time being.

Around the turn of the century the Jeffersons moved to Glasgow, where A.J. took up the post of manager of the local Metropole Theatre. Stan returned to a normal school but preferred to think of his leisure time in the Metropole than listen to his teachers. His father again sent him to another school where he completed his schooling in 1906. His father was not too worried as he still regarded his 16-year-old son as his successor, who he would first make his assistant. But Stan was not so interested in the organisational side of theatre and wanted only one thing: to be a comedian. His great hero was the famous English comic of the time, Dan Leno. But Stan watched lots of other comedians and put together his „own" stage show from the best of their sketches. The premiere was not in his father's theatre but in Albert E. Pickard's cabaret, „Penny Arcade". Pickard was a good friend of Stan's father. As Stan was fully aware of his father's intentions, he first wanted to try out the audience's reaction before attempting to persuade his father that he was more of a comedian than a manager. As chance would have it, Arthur Jefferson went for a walk on that very evening and as he went past Pickard's theatre, the owner offered him a seat, believing he had come to attend his son's opening.

Stan's small stage show appealed to the audience and, at the end of the show, when he spied his father, there

von Stans Vater. Da Stan sich natürlich des Berufs-wunsches bewußt war, den sein Vater für ihn hegte, wollte er zunächst einmal testen, wie er wohl beim Publikum ankäme, bevor er den Vater davon zu überzeugen versuchte, daß er eher zum Komiker als zum Manager taugte. Wie es der Zufall so wollte, machte Arthur Jefferson just an diesem Abend einen Spaziergang, und als er an Pickards Theater vorbei kam, führte ihn dieser zu einem Sitzplatz - in der festen Annahme, der Vater sei gekommen, um der öffentlichen Bühnenpremiere seines Sohnes beizuwohnen.

Stans kleine Bühnenshow kam beim Publikum gut an, und als er am Ende des Programms seinen Vater erspähte, kam es zu einer lustigen, ungewollten Zugabe. Der Knabe stieß nämlich vor Überraschung einen lauten Schrei aus und verbeugte sich hastig, wodurch sein Hut auf den Boden fiel. Als er sich bückte, um den Hut aufzuheben, versetzte er diesem aus Versehen einen Tritt, so daß die Kopfbedeckung in den Orchestergraben purzelte. Stan wollte daraufhin schnell von der Bühne flüchten, doch blieb er hängen und riß sich dabei das Hemd auf. Das Publikum raste angesichts dieser turbulenten Darbietung vor Begeisterung. Viel wichtiger als der Applaus der Zuschauer war für den jungen Stan jedoch, daß sein Vater an der Vorstellung Gefallen gefunden hatte und ihn fortan als Mentor unterstützte.

Durch die Beziehungen seines Vaters fand Stan schon bald einen Platz in der Jugend-Pantomimentruppe „The Levy and Cardwell Juvenile Pantomimes Company", in der junge Talente erste Bühnenerfahrungen sammeln konnten. Stan blieb dort, bis er 19 Jahre alt war, und versuchte anschließend sein Glück mit einem eigenen Soloprogramm auf kleinen Varieté- und Vaudeville-Bühnen in ganz England. Der Vater verhalf ihm zu einem weiteren Karriereschub, indem er ihn zum Hauptdarsteller seiner Vaudeville-Comedy „Home from the Honeymoon" auserkor (dieser Sketch diente Laurel und Hardy Jahre später als Grundlage für zwei ihrer Filme: „Duck Soup" und „Another Fine Mess"). Das Stück wurde ein Riesenerfolg und verschaffte Stan eine große Popularität. In dem Stück „Gentleman Jockey" von 1910 erhielt er seine zweite große Comedy-Rolle am Theater seines Vaters, und noch im selben Jahr wurde Stan von dem Music Hall-Mogul Fred Karno entdeckt. Dieser schickte gleichzeitig mehrere Komikertruppen durch das ganze Land, zum Teil auch in andere europäische Staaten und sogar in die USA. Wer bei Fred Karno unter Vertrag stand, gehörte zu den besten Komikern, die Großbritannien zu bieten hatte.

Stan erhielt seine Chance, und so durfte er 1910 mit einer von Karnos Truppen die Reise über den großen Teich antreten. Star des Ensembles war ein gewisser Charles Chaplin, als dessen Ersatzmann Stan fungierte und mit dem er sich ein Zimmer teilte. Das Stück, mit dem die Truppe unterwegs war, hieß „A Night in an English Music Hall". Chaplins Rolle war es, als Betrunkener aus dem Publikum heraus die Aufführung der

was a funny, unintentional encore. The boy was so surprised that he let out a scream and bowed so quickly that his hat fell onto the stage. As he bent down to retrieve it, he accidently kicked it and the hat fell into the orchestra pit. Then Stan wanted to flee the stage as quickly as possible but became entangled and ripped open his shirt. The audience enthused over this frenzied display, but of more importance to Stan than the audience's applause was that his father liked the show and subsequently supported him as his coach.

Thanks to his father's connections, Stan soon found a place in the Levy and Cardwell Juvenile Pantomimes Company, in which young talent was able to gain its first stage experience. Stan remained there until he was 19 and then tried his luck with a solo performance in small revue and variety theatres throughout England. His father helped him further up the career ladder by choosing him as the lead in his vaudeville comedy, „Home from the Honeymoon" (this sketch was to serve Laurel and Hardy as the basis for two of their films years later, „Duck Soup" and „Another Fine Mess"). The play was a huge success and made Stan extremely popular. In „Gentleman Jockey" in 1910, he gained his second large comic role in his father's theatre and in the same year he was discovered by the great music-hall mogul, Fred Karno. Karno sent several comedy troupes throughout the whole of England, some to other European countries and even to the USA. Whoever was contracted to Fred Karno numbered among the best comedians Great Britain had to offer. Stan was given a chance and went in 1910 with one of Karno's troupes across the Atlantic. The star of this outfit was one Charlie Chaplin, for whom Stan was a stand-in and with whom he shared a room. The play with which the company toured was called „A Night in an English Music Hall". Chaplin's function was to interrupt from among the audience the others' performance in a funny and sometimes crude way. The performance was a huge success and made Chaplin famous. But since Chaplin never fell ill, Stan was not able to prove his own acting ability. And he had hoped to become a star in the US. Thus he became increasingly frustrated with his role as a stand-in. He began to get bored and, since he had never been any good with money, his all too small wage was soon spent. Then, when Karno's tour manager refused him a pay rise, Stan left the troupe, together with the equally discontented Arthur Dandoe.

On the journey back to England, which his father paid for, Stan wrote a sketch for himself and Dandoe entitled „The Rum'uns from Rome". The piece, in which the two played pretty stupid Roman legionaries, turned out to be a huge success on the London stage. But Dandoe was soon offered a better-paid job and Stan was once again left alone. Since he had never wanted to manage his own bookings, Stan quickly joined the comic troupe, The Eight Comiques, who were soon hired for a tour of Holland, Belgium and France. The tour was a flop, since in their first port of call in Rotterdam they were unable

anderen Darsteller auf lustige und teilweise rüde Art zu stören. Die Darbietung war ein großer Erfolg und verhalf Chaplin zu erheblichem Ruhm. Da Chaplin aber nie erkrankte, erhielt Stan keine Gelegenheit, seine eigene Schauspielkunst unter Beweis zu stellen. Dabei hatte er gehofft, in den USA zum Star werden zu können. So machte ihn seine Rolle als Ersatzmann zunehmend unzufriedener. Stan begann sich zu langweilen, und da er noch nie hatte gut mit Geld umgehen können, war die ohnehin niedrige Gage immer schnell ausgegeben. Als ihm dann auch noch eine Gehaltserhöhung von Karnos Tourmanager verweigert wurde, verließ Stan, gemeinsam mit dem ebenfalls unzufriedenen Kollegen Arthur Dandoe, die Truppe.

Auf der Rückreise nach England, die ihm sein Vater bezahlte, schrieb er für sich und Dandoe einen Sketch mit dem Titel „The Rum'uns from Rome". Das Stück, in dem beide ziemlich dämliche römische Legionäre spielten, entpuppte sich auf einer Londoner Bühne als ein schöner Erfolg. Doch Dandoe erhielt kurz darauf ein besser bezahltes Engagement, und so war Stan wieder auf sich alleine gestellt. Da er noch nie große Lust hatte, sich um seine eigenen Theaterbuchungen zu kümmern, schloß sich Stan kurzerhand der Komikertruppe „The Eight Comiques" an, die schon bald für eine Tournee nach Holland, Belgien und Frankreich gebucht wurde. Die Tour war ein großer Mißerfolg, denn schon auf ihrer ersten Station in Rotterdam konnten sie ihre Comedy-Revue „Fun on the Tyrol" nicht aufführen, da das Zelttheater kurz vor der Premiere wegen Baufälligkeit vom Ordnungsamt geschlossen worden war. Und da die Truppe bereits seit Tagen auf Kredit im Hotel geschlafen und gegessen hatte, ging es den Schauspielern schon bald darauf finanziell äußerst schlecht, zumal sie auch von ihrem Vertragspartner kein Geld erhielten. Vom Hunger geplagt und finanziell vollkommen abgebrannt, schlugen sie sich notgedrungen bis ins belgische Lüttich durch. Ausgemergelt, wie sie waren, konnten sie die zum Teil akrobatischen Einlagen ihrer Sketche jedoch nicht durchstehen, so daß sie sich unfreiwillig die ganze Show selbst vermasselten. So blieb den „Eight Comiques" nichts anderes übrig, als sich aufzulösen, und Stan mußte sich widerstrebend bei seinem älteren Bruder Gordon Geld für die Heimreise nach England leihen.

Glücklicherweise wurde Stan jedoch schon bald erneut von Karno für eine Amerika-Tournee verpflichtet. Im Jahre 1912 erhielt Stan eine kleine, aber recht gut bezahlte Rolle, wiederum in dem Stück „A Night in an English Music Hall". Und abermals wurde er von Karno zum Ersatzmann für Charlie Chaplin bestimmt. Nachdem dieser jedoch schon bald vom größten Filmcomedy-Produzenten Mack Sennett für die Leinwand entdeckt wurde, erhielt Stan endlich die Chance, sich als talentierter Hauptdarsteller zu beweisen. Doch zu Stans Unglück identifizierte das Publikum die entsprechende Rolle derart mit der Person von Charlie Chaplin, daß Stan - trotz seines schauspielerischen Talents - von den

to stage their revue „Fun on the Tyrol" as the tent they were to perform in was closed down by the authorities just before the premiere as it was dilapidated. And since the company had been living on credit in a hotel for several days, the actors were soon in financial dire straits, especially as they received no money from their clients. Plagued by hunger and completely broke, they managed to make it to Liège in Belgium. Emaciated as they were, they could not manage some of the acrobatic interludes in their sketches so that they involuntarily ruined their own show. Thus The Eight Comiques had no choice but to disperse and Stan had to force himself to borrow money from his elder brother Gordon for the journey back home to England.

Fortunately, Stan was soon rehired by Karno for a tour of America. In 1912, Stan was given a small but very well-paid role, again in „A Night in an English Music Hall". And once again Karno named him stand-in for Chaplin. However, after the latter was soon discovered for the big screen by the greatest comedy producer, Mack Sennett, Stan finally got the chance to prove he was a talented lead actor. But unfortunately for Stan, the audiences identified the role so much with Charlie Chaplin that Stan was not accepted by them despite his acting talent. Furthermore, since all the theatre owners had booked the Karno troupe mainly due to the star, Charlie Chaplin, they refused to stage the show after Chaplin's departure with the unknown Stanley Jefferson. Fred Karno was then forced to shorten the tour for financial reasons. This was the beginning of 1913 and Stan decided to try his luck in America on his own.

Together with the two former Karno actors Edgar and Wren Hurley, he formed the trio The Three Comiques, who had a fair success with the piece „The Nutty Burglars". The theatrical agent Gordon Bostock saw their performance and helped the three comics get even better bookings with a little trick: Stan was not to break in as a normal burglar but as a copy of the tramp film figure made popular by Chaplin. His stage partners, the Hurleys, slipped into the roles created by Chaplin's film colleagues at that time, Chester Conklin and Mabel Normand. The now „chaplinised" trio changed their name to The Keystone Trio, playing on the name of the Keystone company where Chaplin made his films. After the trio had successfully toured the United States until 1915, it broke up unexpectedly due to a dispute over the leading role and Stan was once again left without a partner.

Yet Stan was soon able to recover from this disappointment by forming the Stanley Jefferson Trio together with the husband-and-wife team Baldwin and Alice Cooke. They toured until 1917 with the piece „The Crazy Cracksman" across the USA with great success, living it up nights and spending their money as fast as they earned it. They often got an advance from their managers, and then forced them to get the trio better bookings if they wanted to see their money again. When

Zuschauern nicht akzeptiert wurde. Da zudem alle Theaterbesitzer die Karno-Truppe hauptsächlich wegen ihres Stars, Charlie Chaplin, gebucht hatten, weigerten sie sich nach Chaplins Weggang, das Stück mit dem unbekannten Stanley Jefferson in ihren Theatern zur Aufführung zu bringen. Dadurch kam Fred Karno in derart arge Bedrängnis, daß er die Tournee aus finanziellen Gründen vorzeitig beenden mußte. Dies war Anfang 1913, und Stan beschloß, von da an sein Glück in Amerika auf eigene Faust zu versuchen.

Gemeinsam mit den zwei ehemaligen Karno-Schauspielern Edgar und Wren Hurley gründete er das Trio „The Three Comiques", das mit dem Stück „The Nutty Burglars" einen schönen Erfolg verbuchen konnte. Der Theateragent Gordon Bostock sah das Stück und verhalf den drei Komikern durch einen Kniff zu noch besseren Buchungen: Stan sollte nicht als gewöhnlicher Einbrecher in ein Haus eindringen, sondern als „Kopie" der durch Chaplin inzwischen überaus populären Filmfigur des Tramp. Seine Bühnenpartner, die Hurleys, schlüpften in die Rollen von Chaplins damaligen Filmkollegen Chester Couklin und Mabel Normand. Das derart „chaplinisierte" Trio änderte seinen Namen kurzerhand in „The Keystone Trio", in Anspielung an die Keystone Company, bei der Chaplin seine Filme veröffentlichte. Nachdem das Trio bis 1915 erfolgreich durch die Vereinigten Staaten getourt war, kam es jedoch im Zuge eines Streits um die Hauptrolle unvermittelt zum Bruch, so daß Stan abermals ohne Partner dastand.

Doch auch von dieser Enttäuschung konnte sich Stan schnell erholen, indem er zusammen mit dem Ehepaar Baldwin und Alice Cooke „The Stanley Jefferson Trio" aus der Taufe hob. Bis 1917 tourten sie mit dem Stück „The Crazy Cracksman" sehr erfolgreich durch die USA, wobei sie stets in den Tag hinein lebten und ihr Geld ebenso schnell ausgaben, wie sie es bekamen. Oft ließen sie sich von ihren Managern sogar einen Vorschuß auszahlen, wodurch sie diese jeweils zwangen, ihnen bessere Engagements zu verschaffen, wollten sie die Vorauszahlung zurückerhalten. Als Stan die australische Sängerin und Tänzerin Mae Dahlberg kennenlernte, war es jedoch wieder einmal um ihn geschehen. Er verliebte sich Hals über Kopf in die neue Bekanntschaft, stieg aus dem „Stanley Jefferson Trio" aus und ging fortan mit Mae auf Tour. Dabei überließ er Baldwin und Alice Cooke die Rechte an seinem Stück und schrieb für sich und seine neue Partnerin einen eigenen Sketch mit dem Titel „No Mother To Guide Them". Da Mae bereits mit einem Australier verheiratet war, der sich partout nicht scheiden lassen wollte, mußten Stan und Mae wider Willen in „wilder Ehe" leben (was sie jedoch nicht daran hinderte, in der Öffentlichkeit als Stan und Mae Jefferson aufzutreten).

Stan then met the Australian singer and dancer Mae Dahlberg it was once again the end for him. He fell head over heels in love with her, left the Stanley Jefferson Trio and went on tour with Mae. He handed over the rights to his play to Baldwin and Alice Cooke and wrote a new sketch for himself and his new partner entitled „No Mother To Guide Them". Since Mae was already married to an Australian who absolutely refused to get divorced, Stan and Mae had to „live in sin" (which did not prevent them appearing in public as Stan and Mae Jefferson).

Bei einem ihrer Auftritte im „Hippodrome Theatre" zu Los Angeles war der Regisseur Adolph Ramish derart von Stan begeistert, daß er ihn spontan für den Film „Nuts in May" engagierte. Bei der Filmpremiere waren sowohl Charlie Chaplin als auch Carl Laemmle, der Chef der Universal Studios, anwesend. Chaplin war von Stans Filmdebüt, in dem dieser einen komischen Kauz mit Napoleonhut spielte, überaus angetan und erwog sogar, ihn für seine eigene Filmproduktion unter Vertrag zu nehmen. Aus heute nicht mehr zu rekonstruierenden Gründen kam dieses Engagement jedoch nicht zustande - hatte Chaplin vielleicht Angst vor zu großer Konkurrenz?

Glücklicherweise war jedoch auch Carl Laemmle von Stan begeistert, so daß er diesem einen Ein-Jahres-Vertrag für die Universal anbot. Die daraufhin produzierten vier Filme, in denen Stan als „Hickory Hiram" agierte, kamen jedoch weder bei Stan noch beim Publikum gut an. Während Stan später immer wieder sagte, die Filme seien schlichtweg schlecht gewesen, sahen andere deren mangelnde Qualität vor allem in Mae Dahlbergs Mitwirken begründet. Als Stans Partnerin hatte sie immer darauf gepocht, eine tragende Rolle in den jeweiligen Filmen zu erhalten. Da es sich bei ihr jedoch ganz einfach um eine schlechte Schauspielerin handelte, kam es zwischen ihr und Stan während der Dreharbeiten immer öfter zum Streit.

Einer der wenigen Augenblicke, den beide relativ friedlich miteinander verbrachten, verhalf Stan eines Tages zu seinem Namenswechsel von Jefferson zu Laurel. Nachdem der Komiker sich schon seit Beginn seiner Filmkarriere über seinen langen Namen geärgert hatte (zum einen hätten ihm die 13 Buchstaben vielleicht Unglück bringen können, zum anderen paßte ein langer Name nur in relativ kleiner Schrift auf Plakate) war nun die Geburtsstunde des Künstlernamens „Laurel" gekommen. Eines Abends stieß Mae beim Herumblättern in einem alten Geschichtsbuch auf eine Zeichnung, in der ein mit Lorbeer (englisch: laurel) bekränzter römischer Feldherr abgebildet war. Sowohl ihr als auch Stan erschien Laurel plötzlich als idealer Ersatz für den eigentlichen Nachnamen Jefferson, und so ist es letztlich dem römischen General Scipio Africanus Major zu verdanken, daß Stan und Ollie nicht als Jefferson und Hardy, sondern als Laurel und Hardy später Weltruhm erlangten.

Stan, der vom Medium Film ohnehin nicht allzu begeistert war, trieb es immer wieder zur Bühne zurück, und so nahm er nur sporadisch Filmrollen an, wenn er gerade keine Theaterbuchungen vorliegen hatte. So drehte er 1918 unter anderem drei Kurzfilme mit Larry Semon, der eher mit spektakulären Stuntszenen als durch hervorragende Schauspielerleistungen glänzte. Da Semon sehr bald merkte, daß ihm der schauspielerisch überlegene Laurel immer mehr die Show stahl, trennten sich die Wege der beiden Komiker schon kurz darauf wieder. Noch im gleichen Jahr kam es zu zwei wei-

During one of their appearances in the Hippodrome Theatre in Los Angeles, the director Adolph Ramish was so impressed by Stan that he hired him on the spot for the film „Nuts in May". Both Charlie Chaplin and Carl Laemmle, head of Universal Studios, were present at the premiere. Chaplin was so taken by Stan's film debut, in which he played a strange fellow in a Napoleon hat, that he contracted Stan for his own film production. For reasons which can no longer be deduced, this never came about - maybe Chaplin was afraid of too much competition.

Fortunately, Carl Laemmle was also impressed by Stan and he offered him a one-year contract at Universal. The resulting four films, in which Stan played Hickory Hiram, were neither a favourite with Stan nor the audiences. While Stan maintained later on that the films were simply bad, others saw the reason for their poor quality in Mae Dahlberg's participation. As Stan's partner, she had always insisted on playing an important role in those films. But since she was quite simply a poor actress, she and Stan quarrelled more and more on the set. One of the few relatively peaceful moments they spent together helped Stan change his name from Jefferson to Laurel. As the comedian had always hated his name since the start of his film career (for a start, the 13 letters could bring bad luck, and furthermore, a long name could only fit on posters in small lettering), it was time for the new pseudonym of Laurel. One evening, Mae was flicking through an old history book when she came across a picture of a Roman general crowned with laurels. This suddenly seemed to both her and Stan to be the ideal replacement for the real name of Jefferson. Thus we have to thank General Scipio Africanus Major that Stan and Ollie later became world famous not as Jefferson and Hardy but as Laurel and Hardy.

Stan, who was not so interested in the medium of film anyway, kept returning to the stage and only took on the odd film role, when he did not have any theatre bookings. In 1918 he made, among other things, three shorts with Larry Semon, who impressed more with spectacular stunt scenes than with brilliant acting. Semon very soon noticed that the superior Laurel increasingly stole the show, and the two comedians soon parted company. In the same year there were two more encounters which were to be important for Stan's later career. He made a few films in the Hal Roach Studios, where he was to become famous years later partnered with Ollie, and for the first time he was to be seen in a film with Oliver Hardy.

In 1918, Hal Roach was looking for a new comic alongside Harold Lloyd. As one of his stars of the time, Toto the clown, had returned to the circus with five films outstanding, Roach quickly hired Stan to finish the productions. Since the films were not particularly successful and Stan was increasingly hitting the bottle (the quarrels with Mae leading to the drinking were no secret to Hal Roach), Stan's contract was not renewed.

teren Begegnungen, die für Stans spätere Karriere von Bedeutung sein sollten. So drehte er einige Filme in den Hal Roach-Studios, in denen er Jahre später im Team mit Ollie berühmt werden sollte, außerdem war er erstmals in einem Film zusammen mit Oliver Hardy zu sehen.

Hal Roach war im Jahr 1918 auf der Suche nach einem neuen Komiker neben Harold Lloyd. Da einer seiner damaliger Stars, der Clown Toto, zum Zirkus zurückgekehrt war, aber noch fünf weitere Filme geplant waren, engagierte Roach kurzerhand Stan, um die entsprechenden Produktionen fertigzustellen. Da die Filme nicht sonderlich erfolgreich waren und Stan zudem des öfte-

Around the same time there was the previously mentioned, historic first encounter between Stan Laurel and Oliver Hardy in the film „The Lucky Dog". Gilbert M. Anderson was the producer, who had been very successful as the western actor Bronco Billy and who went on to become a film producer. In „The Lucky Dog" Stan played the lead while Ollie played the heavy who first wants to rob Stan and then lure his woman away from him. The first sentence which Ollie „said" to Stan on the screen according to the text insert is (holding a gun under his nose): „Put them both up, insect, or I'll comb your hair with lead!" As may be easily seen from this, the two future partners are far removed from the delightful characters who were to find world acclaim.

"THE LUCKY DOG"

A SUN-LITE COMEDY

ren etwas zu tief ins Glas schaute (die dafür verantwortlichen Streitereien mit Mae blieben auch Hal Roach nicht verborgen), wurde Stans Vertrag nicht verlängert.

Etwa zur selben Zeit kam es schließlich in dem Film „The Lucky Dog" zu dem bereits erwähnten historischen ersten Zusammentreffen zwischen Stan Laurel und Oliver Hardy. Als Produzent fungierte Gilbert M. Anderson, der als Westerndarsteller unter dem Namen „Bronco Billy" sehr erfolgreich gewesen war und später selbst als Filmproduzent in Erscheinung trat. In „The Lucky Dog" spielt Stan die Hauptrolle, während Ollie den Bösewicht darstellt, der Stan zunächst ausrauben will und dann auch noch versucht, ihm die Frau abspenstig zu

Stan did not make any more films between 1919 and 1920. Instead he toured on stage across the whole of America and Canada with Mae. In 1921 he made just one film for Vitagraph studios.

Stan's short film excursions up to that time were less than satisfying for both him and the viewers. He had simply not been able to create his own film character for any length of time. He either tried to imitate Chaplin or he played a different character in each new film.

George Stevens, who stood behind the camera in 27 Laurel and Hardy films commented in an interview on Stan's early solo films thus:

machen. Beim ersten Satz, den Ollie laut Texttafel auf der Leinwand zu Stan sagt, hält er ihm eine Pistole unter die Nase: „Heb' sie beide hoch, du Laus, oder ich kämm' dir die Haare mit Blei!" - Wie man aus diesem Satz unschwer erkennen kann, sind hier die beiden späteren Teamkollegen noch weit von den liebevollen Charakteren entfernt, als die sie später zu Weltruhm gelangen sollten.

1919 und 1920 drehte Stan keine weiteren Filme. Stattdessen zog er es vor, gemeinsam mit Mae quer durch Amerika und Kanada auf Theatertournee zu gehen. Im Jahre 1921 drehte er einen einzigen Film in den Vitagraph Studios.

Stans bis dahin kurze Ausflüge zum Film waren sowohl für ihn als auch für das Publikum eher unbefriedigend. Es war ihm einfach nicht gelungen, einen dauerhaften eigenständigen Filmcharakter zu kreieren. Entweder versuchte er, Chaplin zu imitieren, oder er spielte in jedem neuen Film einen anderen Typen.

George Stevens, der bei insgesamt 27 Laurel & Hardy-Filmen als Kameramann und Regisseur mitwirkte, äußerte sich in einem Interview zu Stans frühen Solofilmen wie folgt:

„Bevor Stan zu Roach kam, habe ich ihn einige Male im Film arbeiten sehen und fand, daß er einer der unlustigsten Komiker zu dieser Zeit war. Er hatte immer sehr viel Pomade im Haar und spielte gewöhnlich einen Typen, dem die Doofheit förmlich angeboren war. Für einen Komiker lachte und grinste er viel zu oft. Er brauchte und wollte Lacher so sehr, daß er es zu einer Angewohnheit machte, über sich selbst zu lachen. Es war eine armselige komische Technik (...) Damals suchte er ganz offensichtlich nach einem Erfolgsrezept."

Im Frühling 1922 hatte Stan jedoch das ewige Umherziehen satt und beschloß, es noch einmal - oder besser gesagt: endlich einmal richtig - beim Film zu versuchen.

Er hatte sofort Glück und wurde erneut von Gilbert M. Anderson für insgesamt sechs Filme unter Vertrag genommen, bei denen Anderson selbst Regie führte. Da es zu dieser Zeit sehr populär war, bekannte Filme zu parodieren, wurde Stan von Anderson unter anderem in zwei solchen Parodien eingesetzt. Der erfolgreichere von beiden war „Mud And Sand", eine eigenwillige Interpretation von Rudolph Valentinos dramatischem Stierkampfepos „Blood And Sand". In dem „Remake" tritt Stan als Ruhbarb Vaselino auf. Der zweite Film mit dem Titel „When Knights Were Cold" stellte eine Parodie auf „When Knighthood Was In Flower" mit Marion Davis als Star dar.

Hal Roach, der sich vor allem von diesen Parodien beeindruckt zeigte, köderte Stan mit einem besseren Angebot, so daß er ihn zum zweiten Mal in seine - inzwischen wesentlich größeren - Studios holte. Hal Roach, der die ersten Harold Lloyd-Filme produziert hatte, be-

„Some time before beginning at Roach, I had seen Stan work, and I thought he was one of the unfunniest comedians around. He wore his hair in a high pompadour and usually played a congenital dude or slicker. He laughed and smiled too much as a comedian. He needed and wanted laughs, so much that he made a habit of laughing at himself as a player, which is extremely poor comic technique. How he changed! In those early days he was obviously searching for a fomula."

In the spring of 1922, Stan finally had enough of the continuous moving around and decided once again - or rather, once and for all - to settle into films.

He was lucky straight away and was again contracted by Gilbert M. Anderson for a total of six films, which Anderson himself was to direct. As it was very popular at this time to parody famous films, Anderson used Stan for two such parodies, as well as for other films. The more successful of the two was „Mud and Sand", an unconventional interpretation of Rudolph Valentino's dramatic bull-fighting epic, „Blood and Sand". In the „remake", Stan appears as Ruhbarb Vaselino. The second film, „When Knights Were Cold", was a parody of „When Knighthood Was In Flower" starring Marion Davis.

Hal Roach, who was most impressed by these parodies, enticed Stan with a better offer into his (now much larger) studios for the second time. Roach, who had produced the early Harold Lloyd films before Lloyd became his own producer, also had a huge success with his „Our Gang" films. He intended to invest the resulting profits in further productions, for which Stan seemed to be the right man.

The first films which Stan made for Roach were again parodies of famous works. For example, „Under Two Flags" became „Under Two Jags" and „Monsieur Beaucaire" was „revived" as „Monsieur Don't Care".

Between 1923 and 1924, Stan made over 20 films in the Hal Roach studios. These films were very important for Stan's later career for a number of reasons. Due to the large number of films, he finally had the chance (and, more importantly, the time) to develop his own screen character, which only took on a scanty form to begin with. However, already at this early stage he was developing numerous gags which would be used later in some of the Laurel and Hardy films. Furthermore, Stan learned a lot about film work behind the camera: he occasionally directed, learned how to use a camera, sat in on the editing process and helped develop and write gags.

Thus it was inevitable that he began to become increasingly interested in the medium of film. Since Mae continued to pester him with her acting desires and he again ran foul of Hal Roach, his contract was not renewed and once again he was back on the streets. Here, if not before, he finally realised that Mae, being

vor Lloyd sein eigener Produzent wurde, konnte zusätzlich mit seinen „Our Gang"-Filmen (in Deutschland bekannt als „Die kleinen Strolche") Riesenerfolge verbuchen. Die damit verbundenen finanziellen Erlöse beabsichtigte er in weitere Produktionen zu stecken, für die ihm Stan als der richtige Mann erschien.

Die ersten Filme, die Stan für Roach drehte, waren erneut Parodien auf bekannte Werke. So wurde zum Beispiel der Film „Under Two Flags" zu „Under Two Jags", „Monsieur Beaucaire" erlebte als „Monsieur Don't Care" eine „Wiederaufführung".

the more dominant of the two in their frustrated relationship, was becoming more and more a stone around his neck. But he did not know how to get out of this situation.

In 1925, the producer Joe Rock solved the problem for him. Rock soon noticed that Mae could only hinder Stan's film career and refused to enter into a partner contract (as Mae had stipulated).

In the meantime, word of Stan's problems with alcohol and his relationship had spread through the whole film

Insgesamt drehte Stan 1923 und 1924 über 20 Filme in den Hal Roach-Studios. Diese Filme waren aus mehreren Gründen für Stans spätere Karriere sehr wichtig: Aufgrund der großen Anzahl der Filme hatte er nun endlich Gelegenheit (und vor allem Zeit), einen eigenen Leinwandcharakter zu entwickeln, der zunächst jedoch nur spärlich Formen annahm. Dafür entwickelte er jedoch bereits zu dieser Zeit zahlreiche Gags, die später auch in einigen Laurel & Hardy-Filmen Verwendung finden sollten. Außerdem lernte Stan sehr viel von dem, was neben der eigentlichen Schauspielerei zum Filmen gehörte: Er führte ab und an Regie, lernte mit der Kamera umzugehen, saß im Schneideraum und half beim Entwickeln und Verfassen der Gags.

industry, making it completely impossible for Joe Rock to find a financial backer for his planned series of Laurel shorts. But, since he was convinced of Stan's acting abilities, he decided to finance the pilot film with the title „Detained" himself. At the same time, Mae had to promise never to enter the studios during shooting. Since she kept to her word, Stan really enjoyed the work, so much so that it was not only the pilot film that enjoyed box-office success. The audiences slowly came to identify the Stan Laurel comedies with quality. But as Stan increasingly had to stand in front of the camera with pretty, young women, Mae became more and more jealous and again insisted on being allowed to act with her partner. But by now Rock was finally fed up and

So blieb es nicht aus, daß er sich mehr und mehr für das Medium Film zu interessieren begann. Da ihm Mae nach wie vor mit ihren Schauspielwünschen in den Ohren lag und er dadurch erneut Probleme mit Hal Roach bekam, wurde sein Vertrag nicht verlängert, und prompt saß er wieder einmal auf der Straße. Spätestens zu diesem Zeitpunkt wurde ihm endgültig bewußt, daß Mae als die dominantere Person in dieser verkorksten Beziehung ihm immer mehr zum Klotz am Bein wurde. Doch wußte er nicht, wie er sich aus dieser Lage hätte befreien können.

Im Jahre 1925 nahm ihm der freie Produzent Joe Rock diese Aufgabe ab. Rock merkte schon sehr bald, daß

offered to pay for Mae's return journey to Australia together with a settlement of 1,000 dollars - providing that she would never set foot on American soil again. To everybody's relief, Mae accepted the offer.

So this was how the first of Stan's many frustrated relationships with women came to an end. It was only with his last wife, Ida Kiteva Raphael, that he was to happily spend the last years of his life.

After Mae's departure, Stan seemed to be rid of a great burden. He dived enthusiastically into his work and the resulting films got better and better. But instead of remaining loyal to his „saviour", Joe Rock, Stan decided

Mae für Stans weitere Filmkarriere nur hinderlich sein konnte und ließ sich deshalb auf keinen doppelten Schauspielervertrag (wie er von Mae gefordert worden war) ein.

Stans Alkohol- und Beziehungsprobleme hatten sich unterdessen in der gesamten Filmbranche herumgesprochen, und so fand Joe Rock auch keinerlei Geldgeber für eine von ihm geplante Serie von Laurel-Kurzfilmen. Da er persönlich jedoch von Stans schauspielerischen Fähigkeiten überzeugt war, entschied er sich kurzerhand, den Pilotfilm mit dem Titel „Detained" selbst

in 1925 to accept a more lucrative offer from Hal Roach. Of course, Joe Rock was disappointed about Stan's leaving; after all, he had paved the way to the comic's „personal freedom". On the other hand, he knew that financially he could not compete with Hal Roach's offers. Stan promised Rock that he would only work for Roach behind the camera to begin with. But since Hal Roach needed the talented comic as an actor, it soon led to a legal dispute between Rock and Roach as to Stan's role. However, the case was soon stopped and, at the end of 1926, Rock released Stan so that he could finally work for Roach as a comic in front of the camera (although

zu finanzieren. Gleichzeitig mußte Mae versprechen, niemals während der Dreharbeiten das Studio zu betreten. Nachdem diese sich an das Versprechen hielt, hatte Stan sehr viel Spaß bei der Arbeit, so daß nicht nur der Pilotfilm an den Kinokassen erfreuliche Ergebnisse erzielen konnte. Die Stan Laurel-Comedies wurden beim Publikum allmählich zum Qualitätsbegriff. Doch da Stan im Zuge der Dreharbeiten immer öfter mit hübschen jungen Damen vor der Kamera stand, wurde Mae zunehmend eifersüchtiger und bestand abermals darauf, in den Filmen ihres Lebenspartners mitwirken zu dürfen. Rock allerdings hatte nun endgültig die Nase voll. Er machte Mae das Angebot, ihr die Rückreise nach Australien sowie eine Abfindung von 1000 Dollar zu zahlen - unter der Bedingung, daß sie nie wieder einen Fuß auf das amerikanische Festland setzen würde. Zur Freude aller nahm Mae das Angebot an.

So endete Stans erste von vielen weiteren unglücklichen Beziehungen zu Frauen. Erst mit seiner letzten Frau Ida Kiteva Raphael sollte er glücklich seinen Lebensabend verbringen.

Nach Maes Abreise wirkte Stan wie von einer großen Last befreit, so daß er sich voller Freude auf seine Arbeit stürzte und die dabei entstehenden Filme immer besser wurden. Anstatt jedoch seinem „Befreier" Joe Rock weiterhin treu zu bleiben, entschloß sich Stan 1925, ein finanziell lukrativeres Angebot von Hal Roach anzunehmen. Natürlich war Joe Rock enttäuscht über Stans Weggang, hatte er doch selbst dem Komiker erst zur „persönlichen Freiheit" verholfen. Auf der anderen Seite wußte er auch, daß er finanziell mit den Angeboten Hal Roachs nicht mithalten konnte. Stan versprach Rock, bei Roach zunächst nur hinter der Kamera zu wirken. Da Hal Roach den talentierten Komiker vor allem auch als Schauspieler benötigte, kam es zwischen Rock, Roach und Stan zu einem gerichtlichen Streit um Stans Tätigkeiten. Das Verfahren wurde jedoch sehr bald eingestellt, und Ende 1926 gab Rock Stan frei, so daß dieser bei Roach endlich auch wieder als Komiker vor der Kamera stehen durfte (obwohl ihm seine Anstellung als Gagschreiber und Regisseur mindestens genauso gut gefallen hatte). Mehr oder weniger durch einen Unfall sollte er dann noch im gleichen Jahr mit Oliver Hardy zum zweitenmal vor der Kamera stehen und von da an endgültig Filmgeschichte schreiben.

he enjoyed his position as a gag-writer and director at least as much). It was then more or less by accident that in the same year he was paired with Oliver Hardy for the second time and from then on finally made film history.

Über 1000 Kilometer entfernt von Stans Geburtsort kam es am 18. Januar 1892 im US-amerikanischen Ort Harlem, im Südstaat Georgia, zu einer zwar nicht komplizierten, aber im wahrsten Sinne des Wortes schweren Geburt. Der stramme Knabe wog über 14 Pfund und wurde auf den Namen Norvell Hardy getauft. Mutter Emily war schottischer, der über 18 Jahre ältere Vater Oliver Hardy sen. englischer Abstammung. Sowohl Emily als auch Oliver waren bereits zuvor verheiratet gewesen und brachten eigene Kinder aus ihren ersten Ehen mit (Oliver einen Sohn und zwei Töchter, die alle schon erwachsen waren; Emily je zwei Töchter und Söhne).

Oliver Hardy sen. war ursprünglich Vorarbeiter bei einer Eisenbahngesellschaft gewesen, wechselte jedoch wegen gesundheitlicher Probleme den Beruf und übernahm die Leitung des örtlichen „Turnell Butler" Hotels. Emily hatte trotz eines Kindermädchens alle Hände voll mit der Kindererziehung zu tun, zudem unterstützte sie ihren Mann im Hotelmanagement, wann immer sie konnte. Am 22. November 1892 starb Oliver sen. unerwartet im Alter von 50 Jahren aus bis heute ungeklärten Gründen. Norvell nahm Jahre später, mit Beginn seiner Filmkarriere, seinem Vater zu Ehren dessen Vornamen an und nannte sich fortan Oliver Norvell Hardy. Diesen „verlängerten" Namen sollte er auch später in seinen Tonfilmen mit Stan aufsagen, um seiner Person mehr Würde zu geben - sogar, als ihn der Gefängniswärter in dem Film „Pardon us" danach fragt, um ihn ins Gefängnisbuch einzutragen.

On 18 January 1892, more than 1,000 kilometres away from Stan's birthplace, in Harlem, in the American state of Georgia, a real dumpling was born. The strapping lad weighed over 14 pounds and was christened Norvell Hardy. His mother Emily was of Scottish descent, the father, Oliver Senior, 18 years older than her, of English descent. Both Emily and Oliver Hardy, Sen. had previously been married and had children from their former marriages (Oliver Senior had one son and two daughters, who were already grown up; Emily two sons and two daughters).

Oliver Hardy, Sen. had originally been a foreman with the railway company but had to change his profession for health reasons and took over the local Turnell Butler hotel. In spite of having a nanny, Emily had her hands full bringing up the children, as well as helping her husband with the management of the hotel whenever she could. On 22 November 1892, Oliver Senior died suddenly at the age of fifty, for reasons which are still unknown. Years later, at the start of his film career, Norvell honoured his father by adopting his forename and thereafter called himself Oliver Norvell Hardy. He was to use this extended name in his talkies with Stan, to make his character more dignified - even when the prison officer in „Pardon Us" asks for his name to enter in the prison register.

Der gerade einmal 32jährigen Emily wurde nach dem Tode ihres Mannes zu allem Übel auch noch zu verstehen gegeben, daß ihre Dienste im Hotel nicht mehr gebraucht würden. Emily war jedoch eine willensstarke Frau, die sich so schnell nicht unterkriegen ließ. So kaufte sie sich von den 600 Dollar Hinterlassenschaft ihres Mannes jede Menge Bettwäsche, Geschirr, Besteck und weiteres Hotelinventar, zog in den nahegelegenen Ort Madison und übernahm die Leitung eines kleinen Hotels. Auf sich alleine gestellt mit fünf Kindern, die versorgt werden mußten, hatte sie in den folgenden Jahren mitunter große Schwierigkeiten, die Familie zu ernähren.

Following the death of her husband, Emily, just turned 32, is made to understand that her services in the hotel are no longer required. However, she was a determined woman who was not to be disposed of so easily. With the 600 dollars inherited from her husband she bought a huge amount of bed linen, crockery, cutlery, and other hotel items, moved to the nearby town of Madison and took over the running of a small hotel. All on her own and with five children to support, she found it extremely difficult to feed the family over the next few years.

In contrast to Stan Laurel's family, the Hardys were not a theatrical or show-business family. But Emily enjoyed

Anders als bei Stan Laurels Familie gab es bei den Hardys keinen direkten Bezug zur Schauspielerei oder zum Showbusiness. Emily sang jedoch gerne bei der Arbeit und gönnte sich und ihren Kindern trotz des knappen Geldes hin und wieder den Besuch einer Theater- oder Konzertveranstaltung. So war es nicht verwunderlich, daß sich diese musikalische Begeisterung auch auf ihren jüngsten Sproß übertrug. Der kleine Norwell verfügte über eine schöne Sopranstimme und unterhielt des öfteren die Hotelgäste mit kleinen Gesangseinlagen. Ollies erste Auftritte im Showgeschäft waren somit musikalischer Natur: Er nahm Gesangsunterricht und durfte im Alter von acht Jahren mit der Jugendgesangstruppe „Coburn's Minstrels" auf einer kurzen Tournee durch die Südstaaten reisen.

Um die Jahrhundertwende erfuhr die finanzielle Lage der Hardys durch die Hochzeit der ältesten Tochter Elisabeth eine entscheidende Änderung. Der Vater ihres Bräutigams war ein angesehener Mann im benachbarten Ort Milledgeville, der über gute Beziehungen verfügte. So zog auch Emily mit dem Rest der Familie nach Milledgeville und übernahm im Jahre 1901 das renommierte „Baldwin Hotel". Ollie hatte sich unterdessen neben seinen musikalischen Darbietungen vor Hotelgästen eine weitere Lieblingsbeschäftigung zugelegt: Lobby watching. Er liebte es, in der Hotelhalle zu sitzen und die Leute zu beobachten, die dort ein- und ausgingen. Sein besonderes Interesse galt den zahlreichen Gästen aus der Theater- und Filmwelt. Das zuweilen exaltierte und gekünstelte Verhalten dieser Leute prägte er sich genau ein und imitierte es. Seine letzte Ehefrau Lucille erzählte lange Jahre später einem Reporter, daß Ollie unter anderem auch das übertriebene Niederschreiben seines Namens (wie zum Beispiel in dem Film „Double Whoopee" beim Eintragen ins Hotelgästebuch) von den Gästen aus dem „Baldwin Hotel" abgeschaut hatte.

Auch während seiner Jugendzeit blieb Ollies größte Leidenschaft - neben dem Essen - zunächst die Musik. Er wollte professioneller Sänger werden, und seine Mutter unterstützte ihn bei diesen Plänen; so finanzierte sie dem damals Vierzehnjährigen ein Gesangsstudium am über 100 Kilometer entfernten Musikkonservatorium von Atlanta. Doch anstatt seinen Lehrern zu beweisen, über welch beeindruckende Stimme er verfügte, zog es Ollie vor, dies in einem nahegelegenen Lichtspielhaus vor Publikum zu tun, indem er Diashows mit seinem Sopran untermalte. Als die Mutter davon erfuhr, schrieb sie den verwöhnten Sohn kurzerhand in eine Militärschule ein, um ihm ein wenig Zucht und Ordnung beibringen zu lassen. Doch war der wohlbeleibte Ollie hier bald dem Spott und Hohn seiner Mitschüler ausgesetzt. Zwar verstand er es, seinen Kameraden zuvorzukommen und über seine Körperfülle selbst die besten Witze zu machen, doch die derben Bemerkungen seiner Vorgesetzten machten ihm schwer zu schaffen, so daß er immer noch mehr Süßes in sich hineinschlang. Als er dann auch noch hilflos zuschauen mußte, wie sein Bru-

singing while she worked and treated herself and the children to the occasional theatre or concert trip, despite the lack of money. So it was hardly surprising that her youngest child should be infected by her love of music. Little Oliver had a beautiful soprano voice and often entertained the hotel guests with short musical interludes. Thus, to begin with, Ollie's first steps in show business were of a musical nature. He took singing lessons and, at the age of eight, joined the youth singing troupe „Coburn's Minstrels" on a short tour of the southern states.

Around the turn of the century, the Hardys' financial situation was dramatically altered by the marriage of the eldest daughter, Elisabeth. The bridegroom's father was a respected man in the neighbouring town of Milledgeville and he had good connections. So Emily and the rest of the family moved to Milledgeville and, in 1901, took over the prestigious Baldwin Hotel. Meanwhile, alongside his musical performances, Ollie had acquired another pastime: lobby-watching. He loved sitting in the hotel lobby and watching the people coming and going. He particularly enjoyed watching the numerous guests from the world of film and theatre. He memorised in detail the haughty and artificial behaviour of these people and mimicked it. His last wife, Lucille, told a reporter years later that the exaggerated writing of his name (as in the film „Double Whoopee" when signing the hotel guest book) was one of the things he had learned from the Baldwin's guests.

Even as a teenager, music remained Ollie's greatest passion - alongside food. He wanted to become a professional singer and his mother supported him in this, paying for the fourteen-year-old to take a singing course at the academy of music in Atlanta, 100 kilometres away. But instead of showing his teachers what an impressive voice he had, Ollie preferred to demonstrate this to the audience in a nearby cinema where he accompanied slide-shows with his soprano voice. When his mother learned of this she rapidly sent the prodigal son to military college, to teach him a bit of discipline. However, the corpulent Ollie was soon the butt of his fellow pupils' jokes. He may have known how to beat his peers by making the best jokes about his plumpness himself, but his superiors' cutting remarks got to him, making him stuff himself with even more sweet things. When he could only watch helplessly as his brother Sam drowned in a lake, the weight of this fifteen-year-old edgy boy increased to over 250 pounds and he simply refused to return to the dreaded military college. His mother was sympathetic and, after a further attempt to keep him at a college in north Georgia failed, Ollie was finally allowed to stay with her in Milledgeville. He began by working as an assistant in the local opera house. But when the first cinema opened, he went off immediately to get a job in the „electric theatre". Inspired by the new medium, the adult Oliver was so enthusiastic that within three years he had worked his way up from ticket-

der Sam in einem See ertrank, schnellte das Gewicht des seelisch angeknacksten Fünfzehnjährigen auf über 250 Pfund hoch, und er weigerte sich strikt, weiterhin in diese ungeliebte Militärschule zu gehen. Die Mutter zeigte Verständnis, und nachdem auch ein weiterer Versuch fehlschlug, ihn für längere Zeit auf einem College im Norden von Georgia unterzubringen, durfte Ollie schließlich bei ihr in Milledgeville bleiben. Hier nahm er zunächst einen Aushilfsjob im örtlichen Opernhaus an. Als jedoch das erste Kino eröffnete, versuchte er sofort, eine Anstellung im „Electric Theatre" zu bekommen. Von dem neuen Medium begeistert, engagierte sich der gerade volljährige Oliver so, daß er sich binnen drei Jahren vom Kartenabreißer über den Filmvorführer bis hin zum stellvertretenden Manager hochgearbeitet hatte. Nachdem er Hunderte der überwiegend lustigen Kurzfilme gesehen hatte, kam er zu der Einsicht, daß er das, was die Schauspieler dort auf der Leinwand machten, mindestens genauso gut hinbekäme. Als er vom Aufkommen der Filmindustrie im nahegelegenen Jacksonville erfuhr, entschloß er sich spontan, den guten Job im „Electric Theatre" aufzugeben und sein Glück beim Film zu versuchen.

In Jacksonville verhalf ihm seine gute Singstimme schnell, einen Job als Sänger und Laiendarsteller in kleinen Bühnenshows zu bekommen. Bei einer dieser Shows lernte er die Pianistin Madelyn Saloshin kennen, verliebte sich in die weitaus ältere Frau und heiratete sie schließlich am 17. November 1913 im Alter von 21 Jahren. Durch Madelyns gute Kontakte im Showgeschäft erhielt er bald eine Anstellung bei der Lubin Film Company. Es war zunächst nur ein Aushilfsjob, bei dem Hardy als Mädchen für alles fungierte; abends stand er immer mit Madelyn auf der Bühne und sang. Im April 1914 erhielt er schließlich die erste Chance, sein schauspielerisches Talent unter Beweis zu stellen. Für eine ihrer zahlreichen Kurzkomödien brauchte Lubin Film einen dicken Darsteller, und so wurde Ollie praktisch vom Fleck weg für seinen ersten Film mit dem Titel „Outwitting Dad" engagiert. Der Regisseur zeigte sich von Ollies darstellerischen Fähigkeiten begeistert und vermittelte ihm einen langfristigen, gut bezahlten Schauspielervertrag. Bereits in seinem Filmdebüt verkörperte Ollie, wie in fast allen seiner frühen Solofilme, den „Heavy": den Schurken oder Bösewicht, der dem komischen Hauptdarsteller und dessen Freundin das Leben schwer machte, jedoch am Ende immer der Verlierer war. Meist trug er einen dichten Schnurrbart und hatte buschige Augenbrauen - vom liebevollen Ollie-Charakter war er noch weit entfernt. In dem Film „Outwitting Dad" wurde er als O. N. Hardy aufgelistet; von diesem Zeitpunkt an nahm er offiziell den Vornamen des Vaters an. Ebenfalls zu dieser Zeit bekam er noch einen weiteren Namen, der ihn ein Leben lang verfolgen sollte. Schuld an diesem Spitznamen war der italienische Friseur des Lubin Studios: Jedesmal, wenn er Hardy rasiert hatte, stäubte er etwas Puder auf dessen dicke Backen, klatschte mit der Hand darauf und sagte mit italienischem Akzent: „Nice-a-baby". Schauspiel-

tearer to projectionist to deputy manager. Having seen hundreds of the mainly comic shorts, he came to the opinion that he could do at least as well as the actors on the screen. When he heard about the start of the film industry in nearby Jacksonville, he decided at once to give up his good job at the „electric theatre" and to try his luck in films.

In Jacksonville, his good singing voice soon helped him to get a job as a singer and amateur actor in small stage shows. It was in one of these shows that he met the pianist Madelyn Saloshin, fell in love with this much older woman and then finally married her on 17 November 1913 at the age of 21. Thanks to Madelyn's good contacts in show business he soon got a job with the Lubin Film Company. To begin with, this was just as an assistant, a jack-of-all-trades. By night Hardy then stood next to Madelyn on stage and sang. In April 1914 he finally got his first chance to prove his theatrical talent. A fat actor was needed for one of the numerous Lubin comic shorts and almost straight away Ollie was hired for his first film, „Outwitting Dad". The director was impressed by Ollie's acting ability and secured him a long-term, well-paid acting contract. As early as his film debut, Ollie played the „heavy", as in nearly all of his earlier solo films. The The rogue or scoundrel who makes life difficult for the comic star and his girlfriend but who always loses out in the end. Usually he wore a thick moustache and bushy eyebrows - far removed from the adorable Ollie character. In „Outwitting Dad" he was credited as O.N. Hardy and from this point on he officially took his father's forename. Also at this time he was given another name which was to stay with him until his death. The person responsible for this nickname was the Italian hairdresser at Lubin Studios. Each time he shaved Hardy, he powdered his fat cheeks, slapped them with his hand and said with an Italian accent, „Nice-a-baby". Hardy's fellow actors, who heard this, from then on called him simply „Babe". Even in later solo films and newspaper advertisements the name „Babe Hardy" was used. By August 1915, Hardy had made around 50 shorts for Lubin and had made a name for himself in the entire local film industry as a heavy actor.

When a fire destroyed all the negatives belonging to the Lubin Studios, the company withdrew from the film business. Hardy appeared again for a short time as a singer in various establishments, but was soon made an offer by VIM Comedies Company. In 1916 he found at VIM his first partner in Billy Ruge and together they made more than 30 shorts as „Plump and Runt". At ten minutes in length, the films gave the two little time to develop into a characteristic team. The films were no different from the hundreds of other slapsticks, concerned mainly with wild chases and clobberings. Due to disputes between the two owners of VIM, the studios were dissolved in 1917, but not before Louis Burstein could grab Hardy and other actors for his new King Bee film company.

kollegen, die das mitbekamen, riefen ihn fortan nur noch in der Kurzform „Babe". Selbst in späteren Solofilmen und in Zeitungsankündigungen fiel der Name „Babe Hardy". Bis August 1915 drehte Hardy rund 50 Kurzfilme für Lubin und machte sich schon bald als Heavy-Darsteller in der gesamten Filmbranche der Gegend einen Namen.

Als durch ein Feuer sämtliche Negativ-Kopien der Lubin-Studios vernichtet wurden, zog sich die Gesellschaft aus dem Filmgeschäft zurück. Hardy trat kurzzeitig wieder als Sänger in verschiedenen Etablissements auf, bekam jedoch schon bald ein neues Filmangebot von der VIM Comedies Company. Hier fand er 1916 in Billy Ruge seinen ersten festen Teampartner und drehte mit der Serie „Plump and Runt" mehr als 30 Kurzfilme. Bei den zehnminütigen Filmchen blieb den beiden jedoch wenig Zeit, ein eigenes charakteristisches Paar zu entwickeln. Die Filme unterschieden sich nicht von Hunderten anderer Slapstick-Streifen, bei denen es hauptsächlich um wilde Verfolgungsjagden und Prügeleien ging. Aufgrund von Streitigkeiten zwischen den beiden Eigentümern der VIM-Studios wurden diese 1917 aufgelöst, doch konnte Louis Burstein schon bald Hardy und andere Schauspieler für seine neue Filmgesellschaft King Bee gewinnen.

Ähnlich wie bei Stan Laurel, der zu dieser Zeit immer wieder durch Chaplin-Imitationen aufgefallen war, kam auch Hardy an Chaplin nicht vorbei. Zugpferd der neuen King Bee-Studios war der beste und bekannteste aller Chaplin-Imitatoren, Billy West. Da man Großaufnahmen seines Gesichtes vermied, waren diese Filme tatsächlich kaum von denen Chaplins zu unterscheiden. Hardy, der den Gegenspieler mimte, wurde exakt so geschminkt wie Chaplins Widersacher Eric Campbell - und so hatten die King Bee Studios ein fast identisches Gegenstück zu den erfolgreichen Chaplin-Filmen.

Der Erste Weltkrieg hätte um ein Haar das Ende oder zumindest eine lange Pause für Hardys Karriere bedeutet. Als Amerika 1917 in den Krieg eintrat, wollte sich der patriotische Hardy, dessen Vorfahren treue Diener der Britischen Krone waren, als Kriegsfreiwilliger melden. Er mußte jedoch eine herbe Enttäuschung hinnehmen; der Rekrutierungs-Offizier hatte nur Hohn und Spott für den dicken Hardy übrig. So wurde aus der militärischen Laufbahn Hardys also nichts, dafür konzentrierte er sich umso mehr aufs Filmemachen. Im Oktober 1917 verlegten die King Bee-Studios ihre Produktionsstätten in die Nähe von Hollywood, der aufkommenden Filmmetropole Amerikas.

Im Jahre 1918 wurde die Produktion der Billy West-Filme eingestellt, aber Hardy, der 36 Filme mit West gedreht hatte, fand schnell wieder Arbeit bei anderen Studios. Im selben Jahr kam es im Film „The Lucky Dog" zu einem ersten flüchtigen Aufeinandertreffen mit seinem späteren Teamkollegen Laurel, der ebenfalls erst im Jahr 1917 in Hollywood gelandet war. Zwischen 1919

As with Stan Laurel, who at this time was repeatedly attracting attention due to his Chaplin impersonations, Hardy was also helped along by Chaplin. The crowd-puller at the new King Bee Studios was the best and most famous of all Chaplin impersonators, Billy West. Since no close-ups of his face were used, these films really were almost impossible to distinguish from Chaplin's. Hardy, who mimed Chaplin's opposite, was made up exactly like Eric Campbell and King Bee Studios had an almost identical counterpart to the successful Chaplin films.

The First World War almost meant an end to, or at least a long gap in Hardy's career. When America entered the war in 1917, the patriotic Hardy, whose predecessors were faithful servants to the British crown, wanted to enlist voluntarily. But he was bitterly disappointed: the recruiting officer could only laugh at fat Ollie. Thus nothing became of Hardy's military career, instead he concentrated all the more on making films. In October 1917, King Bee Studios moved their production site to near Hollywood, the blossoming film mecca.

In 1918, production of Billy West films was stopped, but Hardy, who had made 36 films with him, quickly found work with other studios. In the same year he briefly met his future partner Laurel - who also only came to Hollywood in 1917 - in the film „The Lucky Dog". Between 1919 and 1921, Hardy first made a few shorts for L-KO before signing to Vitagraph Studios. Vitagraph had just signed the English comedian Jimmy Aubrey to do a series of shorts and once again Hardy played the heavy.

In his private life, the three years were also eventful for Oliver Hardy. In November 1920, he divorced his first wife Madelyn and almost exactly one year later married the Vitagraph beauty, Myrtle Lee Reeves. Shortly before the marriage, Hardy was given a long-term contract with Vitagraph and was subsequently partnered with Larry Semon, a very famous comic at that time. By now, Hardy was known all over Hollywood as a heavy. In one English film comic there was even a picture story each month with him as the main character, „The Artful Antics of Babe Hardy". Hardy made around a dozen films with Semon until the end of 1923. These were full of fast editing and packed with action. As Semon was more of a stunt man and acrobat than a talented actor, Hardy's dramatic performance was all the more marked. Thus Hardy often stole the show from his partner at that time. As opposed to Laurel, Hardy was never any threat to Semon as he was still the rogue and not the comic.

In the preceding years no role had ever been too small for him. Hardy always tried to make the best of every part. Thus he was able to cultivate his acting ability in over 200 films. Unlike Stan Laurel, who still appears a little nervous in front of the camera later on, Hardy acted with professional coolness and knew how to appeal to the viewer directly.

und 1921 drehte Hardy dann zunächst einige Kurzfilme bei L-KO, bevor er einen längerfristigen Vertrag bei den Vitagraph-Studios erhielt. Diese hatten soeben den englischen Komiker Jimmy Aubrey für eine Kurzfilmserie verpflichtet, und Hardy spielte darin einmal mehr den „Heavy".

Auch privat waren die drei Jahre für Oliver Hardy ereignisreich. Im November 1920 ließ er sich von seiner ersten Ehefrau Madelyn scheiden und heiratete fast genau ein Jahr später die Vitagraph-Schönheit Myrtle Lee Reeves. Kurz vor der Heirat bekam Hardy einen festen Vertrag bei Vitagraph und wurde fortan als Ge-

Hardy and Semon were friends in private too. Semon introduced him to the art of golf, a passion which Hardy succumbed to immediately. Hardly a day went past when he did not play a round of golf after shooting was completed.

Semon's films were very successful, so much so that for some time they were put in the same category as those of Charlie Chaplin and Buster Keaton. Since he was well aware of his popularity, Semon haggled for increasingly high wages and demanded even larger budgets for his already expensive films. Once he and the managers of Vitagraph failed to come to an agreement, the two parted company.

genspieler des damals sehr bekannten Komikers Larry Semon eingesetzt. Hardy war mittlerweile als „Heavy" in ganz Hollywood bekannt; in einem englischen Filmcomic-Heft erschien sogar jeden Monat eine Bildgeschichte mit ihm als Hauptdarsteller: „The Artful Antics of Babe Hardy". Bis Ende 1923 drehte Hardy rund ein Dutzend Filme mit Semon. Dessen Filme waren rasant geschnitten und mit viel Aktion geladen. Da Semon eher ein guter Stuntman und Akrobat als ein begabter Darsteller war, fiel Hardys gute schauspielerische Leistung umso deutlicher auf. So stahl Hardy seinem damaligen Partner des öfteren die Schau. Anders als Laurel war Hardy jedoch kein echter Konkurrent für Semon, da er nach wie vor als Bösewicht und nicht als Komiker agierte.

In den vorangegangenen Jahren war ihm nie eine Rolle zu klein gewesen; Hardy versuchte immer, das Beste

The studios lost their crowd-puller and, after five insignificant shorts, no longer had any use for Hardy. However, Ollie soon found work with the Hal Roach Studios - on a freelance basis at first. Over the next two years he was often used in Hal Roach's famous comedy series with Glen Tyron, Clyde Cook and Charlie Chase. Two of these shorts, „Yes, Yes Nanette" and „Wandering Papas", were directed by Stan Laurel. In the meantime he worked a few times together with Larry Semon again. The latter had by now formed his own production company, Chadwick Pictures, and distributed the self-financed films via the First National film company. Hardy played in some of the full-length features, including „The Perfect Clown", „The Girl in the Limousine" and in Semon's „The Wizard of Oz". However, Semon's poor acting ability was insufficient for these features, which was reflected in the meagre success of the films. Furthermore, Semon overreached himself financially and finally went broke.

daraus zu machen. So entwickelte er in über 200 Filmen sein schauspielerisches Können, das immer perfekter wurde. Im Gegensatz zu Stan Laurel, dem man auch in späteren Jahren noch eine gewisse Nervosität vor der Kamera ansah, agierte Hardy mit professioneller Gelassenheit und verstand es, den Betrachter direkt anzusprechen.

Hardy und Semon waren auch privat befreundet. Semon führte ihn in die Kunst des Golfspielens ein, einer Passion, der Hardy fortan und Zeit seines Lebens verfallen war. Es verging kaum ein Tag, an dem er sich nach Drehschluß nicht noch für eine Runde auf den Golfplatz begab.

Semons Filme waren sehr erfolgreich, so daß diese zeitweise auf eine Stufe mit den Werken Charlie Chaplins und Buster Keatons gestellt wurden. Da er sich seiner Popularität bewußt war, feilschte Semon um immer höhere Gagen und forderte noch größere Budgets für seine ohnehin teuren Filme. Als er mit den Vitagraph-Managern zu keiner befriedigenden Einigung kam, trennte man sich voneinander. Die Studios hatten ihr Zugpferd verloren und nach fünf unbedeutenden Kurzfilmen somit auch keine weitere Verwendung für Hardy mehr. Schon bald fand Ollie jedoch, zunächst auf freier Basis, Arbeit in den Studios von Hal Roach. In den folgenden zwei Jahren wurde er oft in Hal Roachs bekannten Comedy-Serien mit Glen Tyron, Clyde Cook und Charley Chase eingesetzt. In zweien dieser Kurzfilme, „Yes, yes Nanette" und „Wandering Papas", führte Stan Laurel Regie. Zwischendurch arbeitete er auch noch ein paar Male mit Larry Semon zusammen. Dieser hatte inzwischen seine eigene Produktionsfirma, die Chadwick-Pictures, gegründet und ließ die selbstfinanzierten Filme über die First National Filmgesellschaft vertreiben. Hardy spielte unter anderem in den Langfilmen „The Perfect Clown", „The Girl in the Limousine" und in Semons „The Wizard of Oz" mit. Für diese langen Filme reichte Semons schwache schauspielerische Leistung allerdings nicht aus, was sich im mäßigen Erfolg der Filme niederschlug. Zudem übernahm sich Semon finanziell und ging schließlich pleite.

Hardy spielte noch in einigen Filmen für die kleinen Arrow- und Fox-Studios und erhielt schließlich im Februar 1926 einen dauerhaften Vertrag bei den Hal Roach-Studios, denen er mit seinem späteren Teamkollegen Stan Laurel bis 1940 treu blieb. Der Regisseur Leo McCarey war es, der schließlich Hardys komisches Potential entdeckte und ihn dieses nun verstärkt in den Charley Chase-Filmen und den „Kleinen Strolchen" („Our Gang") zeigen ließ. Im Juli 1926 sollte Hardy unter Laurels Regie in dem Film „Get 'em young" eine Nebenrolle als Butler übernehmen. Drei Tage vor Drehbeginn verbrannte sich Hardy jedoch zu Hause beim Zubereiten einer Lammkeule am heißen Fett, zog sich schwere Verbrennungen zu und fiel für einige Zeit aus. Richard Jones, der Produktionsleiter bei Roach, fragte

Hardy made a few more films for the small Arrow and Fox studios and then signed for good to Hal Roach in February 1926, the studios to which he and his future colleague Stan Laurel remained loyal until 1940. It was director Leo McCarey who finally discovered Hardy's comic potential and then used this increasingly in the Charley Chase films and for „Our Gang". In July 1926 Hardy was supposed to play the supporting part of the butler in „Get 'Em Young", directed by Stan Laurel. But three days before shooting started, Hardy burnt himself badly while cooking a leg of lamb in hot fat and was out of action for some time. Richard Jones, the head of production at Roach, then asked Stan Laurel if he did not want to take over the part of the butler. It took a lot of persuasion and a wage increase before Laurel finally agreed to stand in front of the camera after nearly one year's absence. Roach liked Laurel's performance and once Hardy had recovered, a part was written into the script for Stan. In their first films together, the two appear more alongside each other than with each other but slowly the pair developed some of the gags and characteristics which were to be typical later on. Again it was the director and gag-writer, Leo McCarey who first noticed that the two would make a comic team simply because of their physical differences. Thus he gave them increasingly long appearances together in the all-star series. And by the beginning of 1927, the film characters of Laurel and Hardy were finally developed, which were to make them world famous until the end of their lives.

dann Stan Laurel, ob er nicht die Butler-Rolle übernehmen wolle. Es bedurfte einiger Überredungskünste und einer Gehaltserhöhung, bis sich Laurel schließlich bereiterklärte, nach fast einjähriger Abstinenz erneut vor die Kamera zu treten. Roach gefiel Laurels Leistung, und als Hardy endlich wieder genesen war, wurde auch für Laurel fortan eine Rolle ins Drehbuch geschrieben. In diesen ersten gemeinsamen Filmen traten die beiden eher neben- als miteinander in Erscheinung, doch nach und nach entwickelten sie einige für das Team später typische Gags und Charakterzüge. Wiederum war es der Regisseur und Gagschreiber Leo McCarey, dem schließlich als erstem auffiel, daß sich allein schon aus den physischen Gegensätzen der beiden ein komisches Gespann bilden ließ. Und so verschaffte er ihnen innerhalb der „All star"-Serie immer längere gemeinsame Auftritte. Und Anfang des Jahres 1927 waren dann endlich die Filmcharaktere von Laurel & Hardy entwickelt, als die sie zu Weltruhm gelangen und die sie ein Leben lang beibehalten sollten.

Die Hal Roach-Studios

The Hal Roach-Studios

Hal Roach wurde am 14. Januar 1892 in Elmira im Staate New York geboren. Als Neunzehnjähriger verschlug es ihn nach Hollywood, wo er einen Job als Nebendarsteller in Westernfilmen fand. Mit der Zeit wurde er zunächst Regieassistent, arbeitete als Regisseur in den Essanay Studios, wurde Teilhaber einer Filmgesellschaft und machte sich schließlich im Jahre 1919 selbständig und gründete die Hal Roach Studios. Bis auf wenige Ausnahmen wurden hier vor allem Komödien produziert, und es gelang ihm, in den folgenden Jahren einen Stab von hervorragenden Komikern und Regisseuren für sein Studio zu gewinnen. Roach hatte ein Gespür für gute Komik und war immer darauf aus, neue Comedy-Serien zu kreieren. Neben Laurel und Hardy, an deren Zusammenstellung als Paar er nur indirekt beteiligt war, hatte er mit „Our Gang" („Die kleinen Strolche") die erste Kinder-Comedytruppe der Filmgeschichte ins Leben gerufen. Aus seiner Liebe zu Tieren entstand die Serie „Dippy Doo Dads", in der Äffchen neben anderen Tieren in Menschenkleidern und Minidekorationen richtige Spielhandlungen präsentierten.

Durch den großen Erfolg seiner Serien konnte Hal Roach die Studios immer weiter vergrößern, so daß er schnell zum größten Konkurrenten Mack Sennetts (Besitzer der Keystone-Studios) avancierte. Dessen Filme waren reine Actionkomödien, die fast immer nur schnelle Verfolgungsjagden und wilde Klamaukszenen beinhalteten. Der spezielle Stil der Roach-Komödien dagegen war ein viel gemächlicherer; neben Slapstick achtete man vor allem darauf, richtige Charaktere zu entwickeln und dem Ganzen einen logischen Handlungsablauf zu geben. Die Filme wirkten dadurch viel realistischer und vor allem menschlicher als die wirren Slapstick-Komödien Sennetts. Ausschlaggebend für den Erfolg der Roach-Produkte war die Arbeitsatmosphäre, die in dem kleinen Studio herrschte. Bei den Dreharbeiten ging es stets familiär und ungezwungen zu. Anders als bei den großen Filmproduktionsstätten gab es hier keine strikten Regeln. Es wurde sehr viel improvisiert, und anstatt umfangreiche Drehbücher zu schreiben, entwickelten die Verantwortlichen die Szenen häufig spontan auf dem Set. Wenn überhaupt, gab es zuvor jeweils nur eine kurze Idee für den Inhalt der Filme. Bis auf Stuntszenen wurde selten geprobt, da man immer den Zauber des ersten Mals einfangen wollte. Roach achtete darauf, daß jeder seiner Mitarbeiter nicht nur eine einzelne, bestimmte Aufgabe übernahm, sondern auch in anderen Arbeitsbereichen tätig war. So gab es neben Stan noch andere Schauspieler, die auch hin und wieder Regie führten. Jeder, der eine bestimmte Fähigkeit besaß, wurde entsprechend gefördert. Wenn beispielsweise ein Beleuchter eine Idee für einen guten Gag hatte, konnte er diese frei vortragen. Alles beherrschende Regisseure, wie in den großen Studios, gab es bei Roach nicht. Man war eine große Familie: Die Mitarbeiter mochten Roach, und umgekehrt war es genauso. Durch dieses Arbeitsklima beflügelt, drehten auch Laurel und Hardy dort ihre besten Filme.

Hal Roach was born on 14 January 1892 in Elmira in New York State. At the age of nineteen he went off to Hollywood, where he found a job as a supporting actor in westerns. As time went on, he worked his way up first as an assistant director, then as a director for Essanay Studios, became a partner in a film company and, in 1919, finally became independent and formed the Hal Roach Studios. Apart from a few exceptions, these only produced comedies and over the next few years he was able to put together a small team of excellent comedians, directors and gag-writers. Roach had a nose for good comedy and was always on the look-out for new comedy series. Alongside Laurel and Hardy, a partnership for which he was only partly responsible, he created the first children's comedy troupe in film history - „Our Gang". His love of animals led to the series „Dippy Doo Dads", in which chimps and dogs, as well as other animals, in human clothing played out real stories on mini-sets.

Thanks to the huge success of his series, Hal Roach was able to constantly expand his studios, quickly becoming Keystone-owner Mack Sennett's biggest rival. Sennett's films were pure action-comedies which nearly always contained fast chases and wild slapstick scenes. Roach's comedies, on the other hand, had a much more leisurely style. Apart from the pure slapstick, attention was paid to developing real characters and giving the whole film a logical plot. This meant that the films seemed much more realistic and, above all, more human than Sennett's crazy slapsticks. Of major importance for the success of the Roach productions was the working atmosphere prevalent in the small studios. On the set, things were done informally and without constraints. As opposed to the large film studios, there were no strict rules and regulations. Much was improvised and instead of writing comprehensive scripts, the scenes were often developed spontaneously on the set. Before shooting started, there was usually only one simple idea for the plot of a film, if there was one at all. Apart from stunt scenes, there was little rehearsal as Roach wanted to capture that magic first time. He made sure that none of his staff only took on one task, but that they were involved in other fields too. Thus Stan was not the only actor to direct now and again. Every one with a certain talent was accordingly encouraged. If, for example, a lighting man had an idea for a gag, he was free to put it forward. There were no omnipotent directors at Roach's studios, unlike at many of the large studios. It was one large family. The staff liked Roach and vice versa. Inspired by this working atmosphere, Laurel and Hardy made their best films.

Stans und Ollies Lieblingsfeinde

Stan und Ollie's pet hates

Laurel und Hardy drehten in ihrer kreativsten Schaffensperiode fast sämtliche Filme in den Hal Roach-Studios. Dem Umstand, daß sie einem einzigen Studio so lange die Treue hielten, ist es zu verdanken, daß ihre Filme eine gewisse Kontinuität aufweisen. Hier hatten Stan und Ollie Zeit, in Ruhe ihre Filmcharaktere zu entwickeln. Die wenigen Gebäude und Straßenkulissen der Hal Roach-Studios sowie -Wohnungssets tauchten immer wieder auf, und so fühlten sich auch die Betrachter der jeweiligen Filme oft „zu Hause". Das wichtigste bei dieser Kontinuität war, daß auch die Nebendarsteller (und vor allem die Laurel und Hardy-Gegenspieler) häufig über Jahre hinweg immer dieselben blieben und so zu einem festen Bestandteil der Filme wurden. Diese Hal Roach Stock Company hatte einen großen Anteil am Erfolg der Laurel und Hardy-Filme und der zahlreichen anderen Roach-Comedyserien. Zwei ihrer besten und beim Publikum beliebtesten Widersacher waren sicherlich der kleine Charlie Hall und der glatzköpfige, schnauzbärtige James Finlayson.

Laurel verhalf auch einigen ehemaligen Freunden aus seiner Theater- und Solofilmzeit zu einer Anstellung bei Roach. So stammte beispielsweise Charlie Hall aus derselben Fred Karno-Theatertruppe, mit der auch Laurel nach Amerika gekommen war. Er erhielt nie eine Hauptrolle bei Roach, doch aus den vielen kleinen Rollen, die er in den Laurel und Hardy-Filmen übernahm, machte er jeweils das Beste. So war er derjenige, der auf Stans weggeworfener Bananenschale ausrutschte und daraufhin mit Stan und Ollie die größte Tortenschlacht der Filmgeschichte auslöste (in „The Battle of the Century"). Einen bleibenden Eindruck hinterließ er jedoch vor allem durch zwei andere Filme: In „Them Thar Hills" demolierte er Stan und Ollies Wohnwagen, in „Tit for Tat" machte er sich äußerst rabiat an Stan und Ollies neu eröffnetem Elektroladen zu schaffen. Hall war in insgesamt 47 Laurel und Hardy-Filmen zu sehen.

Der beim Publikum beliebteste aller Laurel und Hardy-Mitspieler war jedoch der schottische Schauspieler James „Fin" Finlayson mit insgesamt 33 Auftritten. Er war aber nicht bloß der „reine Finsterling", sondern auf eine witzige Art unsympatisch. Die Person, die er jeweils verkörperte, konnte cholerisch, aggressiv und hinterhältig sein, blieb dabei aber immer komisch. Er war bereits des öfteren in Stans Solofilmen für Roach zu sehen gewesen und war einer der „All Stars", mit denen zusammen auch Laurel und Hardy ihre ersten gemeinsamen Filme machten. Der sicherlich bekannteste Film, den er mit den beiden drehte, war „Big Business". Stan und Ollie, die ihm hier einen Weihnachtsbaum an der Haustür verkaufen wollen, werden von Fin barsch abgewiesen. Dabei eskaliert ein anfänglich harmloser Streit zwischen den dreien zu einer regelrechten Orgie der Verwüstung, in deren Verlauf Laurel und Hardys Lieferwagen sowie Fins Haus aufs ärgste demoliert werden.

During their most creative period, Laurel and Hardy made nearly all their films in the Hal Roach studios. It is due to the fact that they remained loyal to one studio for so long that their films have a certain continuity. Stan and Ollie had the time and space here to develop their screen characters. The few buildings and street and interior sets in the Hal Roach studios are used again and again, so that the viewer often felt at home watching the films. The most important part of this continuity was that the supporting actors (especially Laurel and Hardy's opposites) often remained the same over many years and so became an essential part of the films. This Hal Roach Stock Company was responsible for a large amount of the success of the Laurel and Hardy films and the numerous other Roach comedy series. Two of their best and most popular among audiences were without doubt little Charlie Hall and the bald-headed, moustached James Finlayson.

Laurel helped some of his former friends from his stint in theatre and solo films get jobs with Roach. For example, Charlie Hall belonged to the same Fred Karno troupe which brought Laurel to America. He never got a leading part with Roach but always made the best out of all the small roles he took on in Laurel and Hardy films. Thus it was he who slipped on Stan's discarded banana skin and started the biggest custard-pie fight in the history of cinema („The Battle of the Century"). But he made a lasting impression in two other films. He demolished Stan and Ollie's caravan in „Them Thar Hills" and in „Tit for Tat" he got furiously to work on Stan and Ollie's newly-opened electrical goods store. In total, Hall appeared in 47 Laurel and Hardy films.

However, the audiences' number-one favourite among the Laurel and Hardy supporting actors was the Scottish actor, James „Fin" Finlayson, who appeared in 29 films. He was not just a pure sinister character but was unpleasant in a funny sort of way. His character could be bad-tempered, aggressive and cunning, but always remained funny. He had already appeared several times in Stan's solo films for Roach and was one of the all-stars with whom Laurel and Hardy made their first films together. Without doubt the most famous film he made with them was „Big Business". Stan and Ollie ring at his door to sell him a Christmas tree and are rudely sent packing by Fin. What begins as a harmless quarrel then escalates into an orgy of destruction in which both Laurel and Hardy's delivery van and Fin's house are horrendously destroyed.

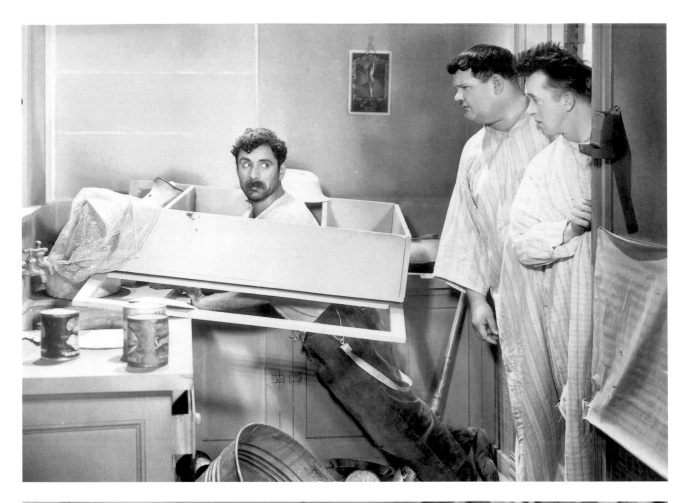

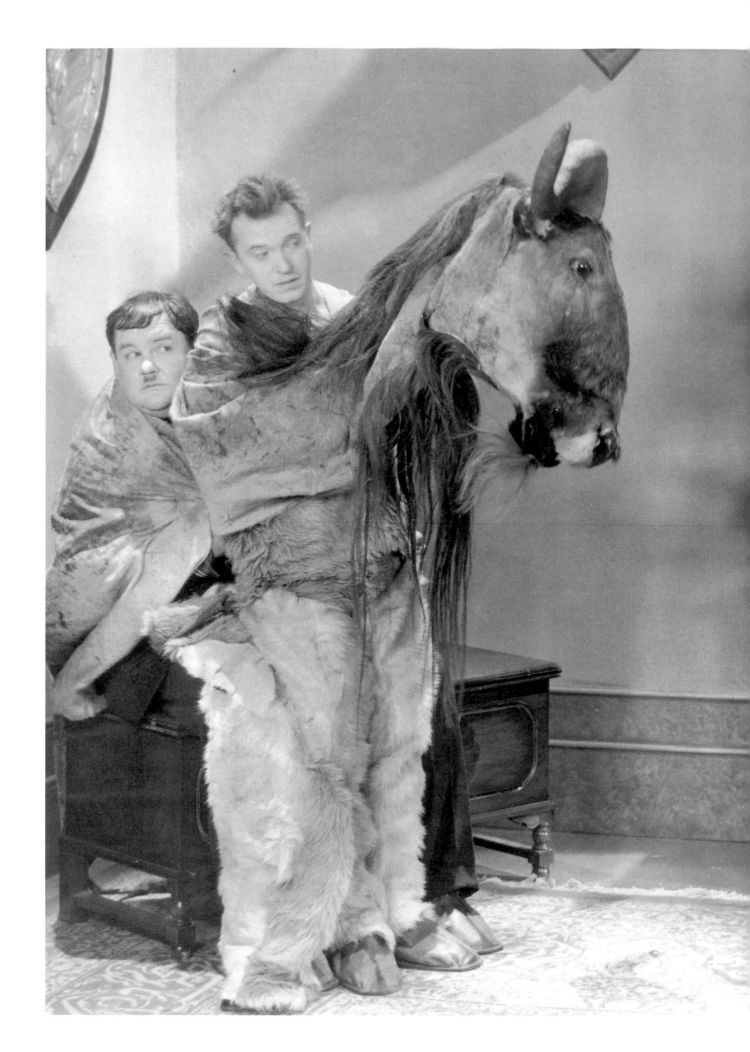

Stan und Ollie sprechen ausländisch
Stan and Ollie talk abroad

Stan und Ollie
sprechen ausländisch

Anfang der dreißiger Jahre trat der Tonfilm seinen weltweiten Siegeszug an. Für viele Stars der auslaufenden Stummfilm-Ära bedeutete der Ton das Ende ihrer Leinwandkarriere, da sie entweder über keine ausdrucksvolle Stimme verfügten oder diese ganz einfach nicht zu ihrem bisherigen Filmcharakter paßte. Da die meisten Roach-Schauspieler von der Bühne stammten, hatten diese mit dem Ton keine Probleme. Auch die Stimmen von Laurel und Hardy paßten glücklicherweise optimal zu ihren Charakteren, außerdem vertrauten Stan und Ollie auch weiterhin auf ihre pantomimischen Fähigkeiten; Dialog setzten sie nur unterstützend und recht sparsam ein, wobei die Tonspur oft hauptsächlich für wirkungsvolle Geräuscheffekte genutzt wurde. Da es anfangs noch keine Synchronisation gab, entschied sich Hal Roach, wie einige große Studios auch, fremdländische Sprachfassungen der Filme seiner beliebtesten Stars herzustellen. Die Nebendarsteller wurden aus den jeweiligen Ländern engagiert. Lediglich die Hauptdarsteller waren natürlich nicht zu ersetzen. So erhielten Laurel und Hardy Sprachunterricht, wobei ihnen die Dialog-Sätze zusätzlich in phonetischer Schrift auf großen Tafeln neben die Kamera gehalten wurden. Da weder Laurel noch Hardy einer Fremdsprache mächtig waren, hatten sie es nicht leicht, die Aussprache so hinzubekommen, daß die Zuschauer der einzelnen Länder sie auch verstehen konnten. Doch waren die Sprachlehrer sehr geduldig, außerdem verlieh Stan und Ollies starker amerikanischer Akzent den Fremdfassungen einen zusätzlichen komischen Effekt. Das ausländische Publikum dankte es ihnen, mußte es doch auf diese Weise keine langen Untertitel lesen. Insgesamt wurden acht Laurel und Hardy-Kurzfilme sowie ihr erster Langfilm („Pardon us") in - teilweise bis zu vier - fremdsprachigen Fassungen gedreht. Die meisten solcher Versionen wurden auf spanisch gedreht, außerdem mindestens zwei auf italienisch, sechs auf französisch und drei auf deutsch.

Der Aufwand lohnte sich zunächst auch, da Roach vor allem auf dem südamerikanischen Markt die Kurzfilme zu Langfilmpreisen verkaufen konnte. Die italienischen und deutschen Fassungen gelten heute leider als verschollen, und so kann man nur erahnen, wie Stan und Ollie mit der richtigen deutschen Aussprache zu kämpfen hatten. Alle spanischen und einige französische Fassungen existieren heute noch. Dabei ist das Besondere, neben der wirklich komischen Aussprache, daß die Filme um viele Szenen erweitert wurden, die in den amerikanischen Orginalfassungen gar nicht enthalten waren. Der erste fremdsprachige Laurel und Hardy-Film war „Night Owls", der letzte „Chickens Come Home". Ab 1932 wurden die Filme dann aus Kosten-, vor allem aber auch aus Zeitgründen nur noch synchronisiert oder untertitelt. Deutsche Versionen gab es von „Brats" („Glückliche Kindheit"), von „The Laurel and Hardy murder case" („Spuk um Mitternacht") und von „Pardon Us" („Hinter Schloß und Riegel").

Stan and Ollie's
talk abroad

The start of the 1930s saw sound films begin their triumphant march across the globe. For many stars of the silent film era, sound meant the end of their film career, as they either did not have an expressive voice or their voice simply did not match their character. Hal Roach was already prepared for the production of talkies before the great MGM studios were. Since most of his actors came from the world of theatre, they did not have any problems with sound. Fortunately, Laurel and Hardy's voices, too, perfectly matched their characters. Furthermore, they still relied on their pantomime talents and only used speech additionally and sparingly, mainly leaving the soundtrack free for dramatic sound effects. Since in the beginning there was no dubbing, Hal Roach, like some of the other large studios, decided to make foreign-language versions of the films with his most popular stars. The supporting actors were recruited from the relevant countries. But of course the leading actors could not be replaced. Thus Laurel and Hardy were given language lessons, and their dialogue was written with phonetic pronunciation on large boards next to the camera. Since neither Laurel nor Hardy spoke any foreign languages, they did not find it easy to pronounce the text in such a way that the foreign audiences would understand them. But their language teachers were very patient and Stan and Ollie's heavy American accents gave the films an additional comic touch. The foreign audiences were grateful that they then did not have to read long subtitles. In total, eight Laurel and Hardy shorts as well as their first feature („Pardon Us") were made in up to four different foreign-language versions. Most of them were in Spanish, at least two were in Italian, six in French and three in German.

Initially it was worth the effort as Roach was able to sell the shorts at feature-film prices in South America. Unfortunately, the Italian and German versions are believed to be lost and so we can only imagine how Stan and Ollie must have fought with the German pronunciation. All of the Spanish and some of the French versions are still in existence. What is particularly interesting (apart from the really funny accents) is that the films were lengthened by several new scenes which were not in the original American versions. Often two shorts were edited together with some new scenes to make one full-length feature. The first foreign-language Laurel and Hardy film was „Night Owls", the last „Chickens Come Home". From 1932 onwards, the films were then dubbed or subtitled to save money but, above all, time. German versions were made of „Brats" („Glückliche Kindheit"), „The Laurel and Hardy Murder Case" („Spuk um Mitternacht") and „Pardon Us" („Hinter Schloß und Riegel").

HRL30-HFR

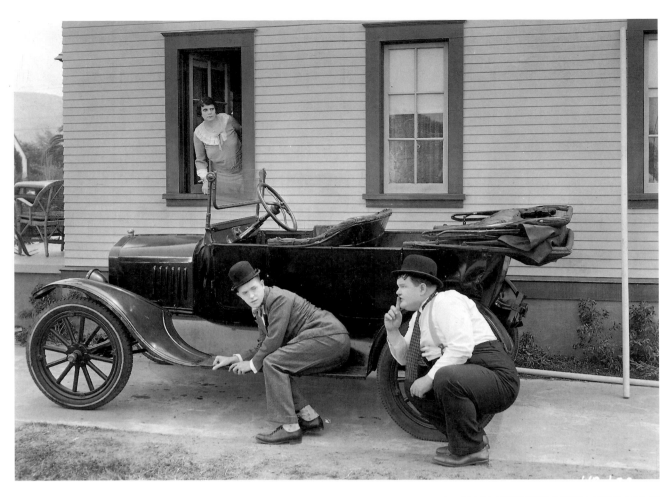

HR-L33-19FR

Seite 52
Gagfoto von 1929

Page 52
Gagshot from 1929

Seite 54
Oben:
Stan in einer Szene die nur in den
fremdsprachigen Fassungen von
„Be Big" vorkommt, 1931

Unten: (sowie Seite 55)
Szenenfotos der französischen Fassung
von „Blotto" mit Georgette Rhodes,
1930

Page 54
Above:
Stan in a scene which only appeared
in the foreign versions of „Be Big", 1931

Bottom: (as on page 55)
stills from the French version of
„Blotto" with Georgette Rhodes, 1930

Seite 56
Szenenfotos der spanischen Fassung
von „Below Zero" mit Bob O'Connor
als Polizist

Page 56
Stills from the Spanish version of
„Below Zero" with Bob O'Connor
as the policeman

Seite 57
Ollies amerikanische Ehefrau
Fay Holderness (oben) in „Hog Wild",
1930, die durch Georgette Rhodes
(unten sowie Seite 58/59) in der
französichen Fassung ersetzt wurde.

Page 57
Ollie's American wife Fay Holderness
(top) in „Hog Wild", 1930, who was
replaced by Georgette Rhodes
(bottom and page 58/59) in the
French version

Doppelter Schlamassel

In dreien ihrer Filme für Hal Roach sind Laurel und Hardy in Doppelrollen zu sehen. Zwar sind die Filme dadurch nicht unbedingt doppelt so lustig geraten, doch bieten sie eine schöne Abwechslung zu ihrer üblichen „Zweisamkeit". Der erste Film dieser Art war „Brats". Hier spielen Stan und Ollie sich und ihre beiden Söhne. Die süßen Sprößlinge wurden dabei nicht etwa tricktechnisch verkleinert, sondern in einem um das Dreifache vergrößerten Riesenset gefilmt (während die Väter in einem identischen, aber normal großen Set agierten). Drei dieser „Riesen-Kulissen" wurden mit viel Liebe zum Detail aufgebaut: Im Wohnzimmer spielen die Kleinen zunächst mit riesigen Bauklötzen, im Kinderzimmer wartet ein Riesen-Bett auf die beiden, während im Badezimmer schließlich Ollie durch Stans Schuld in eine bis zum Rand mit Wasser gefüllte Riesen-Badewanne plumpst. Anders als auf einem der nebenstehenden Fotos (bei dem es sich um eine Fotomontage handelt), sind die beiden Paare auf der Leinwand niemals gleichzeitig zu sehen.

Dies war drei Jahre später in dem Film „Twice Two" der Fall, in dem Stan und Ollie sich sowie ihre eigenen Ehefrauen spielen. Hier war es durch eine Doppelbelichtung des Filmmaterials möglich, beide Paare tatsächlich gleichzeitig auf die Leinwand zu bannen. Dies geschah, indem zunächst eine Hälfte des Kamera-Objektivs zugehalten und anschließend der zurückgespulte Film auf der anderen Seite belichtet wurde. Verantwortlicher Kameramann damals war Art Lloyd, der ein Jahr später diese Tricktechnik in dem Charley Chase-Film „Four parts" auf die Spitze treiben sollte (hier sind in einer Szenen Vierlinge, alle von Chase gespielt, gleichzeitig zu sehen). Hatte Stan schon vor „Twice Two" des öfteren Frauenrollen gespielt, so schlüpft Ollie hier das erste und einzige Mal in die Rolle des anderen Geschlechts. Dabei präsentiert uns Ollie auch hier die dominantere Ehefrau, die ständig unter Stans Mißgeschicken leidet. Die Frauenstimmen der beiden Komiker wurden nachsynchronisiert (von Carol Tevis für Stan und May Wallace für Ollie). Doch während Ollies Stimme so klingt, wie man sich Ollie als Frau tatsächlich vorstellen könnte, ist Stans Organ übertrieben piepsig geraten und teilweise schwer zu verstehen.

Im dritten und zugleich einzigen Langfilm, in dem Stan und Ollie in Doppelrollen zu sehen sind, spielen sie sich sowie ihre beiden Zwillingsbrüder Bert (Hardy) und Alf (Laurel) in „Our Relations". Bert und Alf sind Matrosen, die ihre Brüder seit frühester Kindheit nicht mehr gesehen haben und nun zufällig in dem gleichen Ort vor Anker gehen, in dem Stan und Ollie ein vergleichsweise biederes Leben mit ihren Frauen führen. Das Hauptaugenmerk ist hier jedoch nicht etwa auf die Tricktechnik gelegt (so sind lediglich in der Schlußszene für kurze Zeit einmal alle vier Zwillinge gleichzeitig zu sehen); der Film ist ganz einfach nicht mehr und nicht weniger als eine wunderschöne, von Kameramann Rudolph Maté hervorragend ins Bild gesetzte Verwechslungskomödie.

Double trouble

In three of their films for Hal Roach, Laurel and Hardy may be seen in double roles. The films may not be twice as funny, but they offer a grand alternative to the usual twosome. The first film of this type was „Brats". Stan and Ollie play themselves as well as their two sons, also called Stan and Oliver. The sweet children were not reduced by clever editing tricks but were filmed on a huge set, three times normal size (while the fathers played on an identical, but normal-sized set). Three of these giant sets were lovingly created: to begin with, in the living room we find the little ones playing with huge building bricks, a huge bed awaits them in the nursery, while in the bathroom Ollie, thanks to Stan, ends up falling into a huge bathtub filled to the brim. As opposed to the photo shown here (which is a montage), the two pairs are never seen together on the screen.

This was, however, the case three years later in the film „Twice Two", in which Stan and Ollie played themselves as well as their wives. By double exposing the film, it was possible to show both couples on the screen at the same time. This was done by first covering one half of the camera lens and then winding back the film to be exposed on the other side. The cameraman responsible at that time was Art Lloyd, who, one year later, was to push this trick to its extremes in the Charlie Chase film „Four Parts" (where in one scene we see quadruplets all played by Chase). Whereas Stan had often played women prior to „Twice Two", Ollie slipped here for the first and last time into the role of the opposite sex. Even here, Ollie plays the more dominant of the two wives, constantly having to suffer Stan's calamities. The female voices of the two were dubbed (by Carol Tevis for Stan and May Wallace for Ollie). But while Ollie's voice sounds as one would imagine Ollie to sound as a woman, Stan's is exaggeratedly squeaky and sometimes difficult to understand.

In the third and only feature film in which Stan and Ollie are to be seen in double roles („Our Relations"), they play themselves as well as their twin brothers Bert (Hardy) and Alf (Laurel). Bert and Alf are sailors who have not seen their brothers since early childhood and now happen to anchor in the same place where Stan and Ollie lead relatively bourgeois lives together with their wives. The main attraction here, however, is not the tricks (all four twins are seen only briefly in the final scene), but that the film is nothing more and nothing less than a wonderful comedy of mistaken identity, brilliantly filmed by the cameraman Rudolph Maté.

HR-L12-7

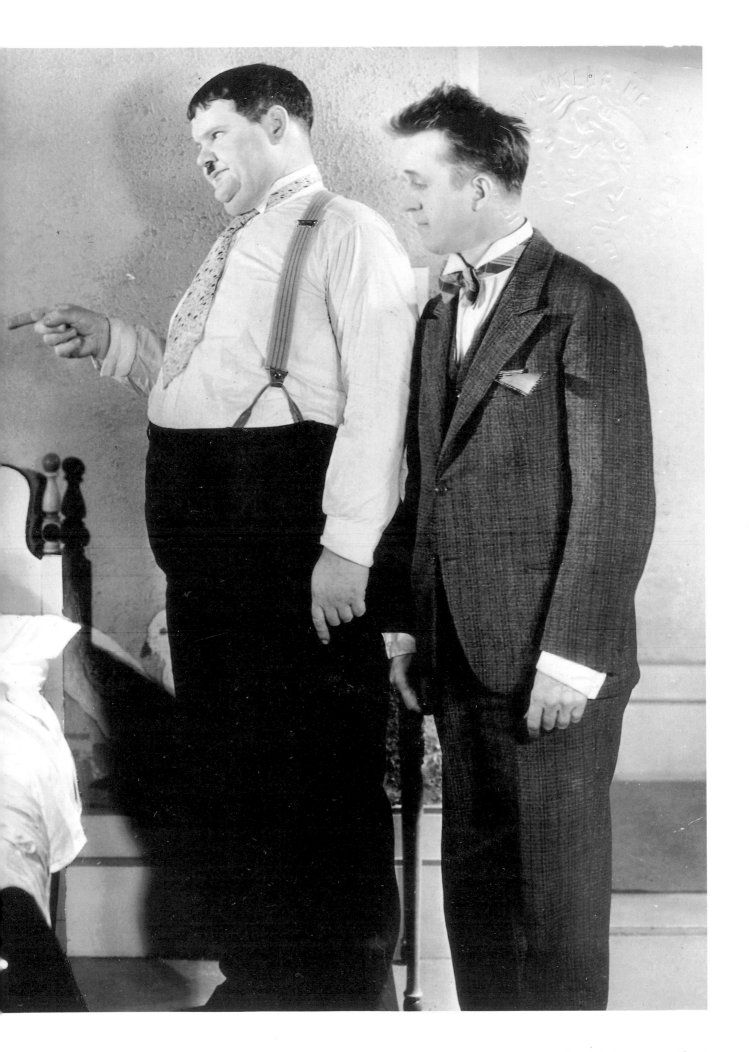

Lachopern

Im Jahr 1929 drehte die MGM unter großem Aufwand und in Zweifarb-Technicolor das Opernepos „The Rogue Song" mit dem damaligen Opernstar Lawrence Tibbett in der Hauptrolle. Da der Film während der Vorpremiere beim Publikum nicht allzu gut ankam, lieh sich MGM kurzerhand bei Hal Roach Laurel und Hardy aus, um mit ihnen nachträglich ein paar lustige Szenen zu drehen. Leider gilt der Film bis heute als verschollen. Laurel und Hardys erster und zugleich bester eigener Schritt in die Opernverfilmung war „The devil's brother", eine Parodie auf Aubers lustige Oper „Fra Diavolo". Der Film spielt im Italien des 18. Jahrhunderts; Stanlio und Ollio müssen zwangsweise den galanten Gauner Fra Diavolo bei einem seiner Beutezüge unterstützen, wobei sie ihm das Vorhaben natürlich gründlich vermasseln. Die Höhepunkte des Films sind (neben der wohl gelungensten aller ihrer Lachszenen) Stans groteske körperlichen Fähigkeiten: Das „Fingerwinken" und das komplizierte „Kniechen-Näschen-Öhrchen"-Spiel, welches nicht nur Ollio, sondern auch viele Zuschauer beim Versuch der Nachahmung zur Verzweiflung trieb.

In Victor Herberts (im wahrsten Sinne des Wortes) märchenhafter Operettenverfilmung „Babes in Toyland" arbeiten Stan und Ollio in einer Spielzeugfabrik und retten am Schluß das von dem Schurken Barnaby bedrohte Spielzeugland. Da hier auch der Weihnachtsmann eine Rolle spielt, läuft der Film alljährlich zum Weihnachtsfest auf unzähligen amerikanischen Fernsehkanälen.

Die dritte Opernverfilmung spielt, wie der Titel „The Bohemian Girl" bereits erkennen läßt, im Böhmen des 18. Jahrhunderts. Stan und Ollio agieren als umherziehende Zigeuner, denen ein Baby in den Pferdewagen gelegt wird, um das sie sich in der Folge rührend kümmern. Wie sich am Ende des Films herausstellt, handelt es sich bei dem Mädchen um die totgeglaubte Tochter eines reichen Grafen. Zum Schluß des Films kommt es jedoch keineswegs zum happy end, sondern zu einer für Laurel und Hardy typischen, skurrilen Szene: Ollio wird durch die Streckbank um zwei Meter „verlängert", Stan hingegen durch eine Presse zum Zwerg verkleinert.

Der Operettenfilm „Swiss Miss" bildet den Schluß und zugleich Tiefpunkt auf Laurel und Hardys musikalischen Wegen. Hier sind sie in der Schweiz als Mausefallen-Verkäufer unterwegs, die in arge Schwierigkeiten geraten und zur Zwangsarbeit in einem Alpenhotel verdonnert werden. Insgesamt läßt sich sagen, daß die Opernfilme durch die schönen Kostüme und aufwendigen Dekorationen einen besonderen Reiz besitzen und eine originelle Abwechslung zu den sonstigen Laurel und Hardy-Filmen darstellen. Durch die langen Gesangseinlagen anderer (Stan und Ollio singen insgesamt leider nur zweimal selbst) erhalten die Werke, wie auch viele ihrer anderen Langfilme, jedoch zuviel Nebenhandlung, so daß trotz mancher lustigen Szene die Komik insgesamt oft auf der Strecke bleibt.

Comic operas

In 1929 MGM filmed at great expense and in Technicolor the operatic epic „The Rogue Song" with the operatic star of the time, Lawrence Tibbett, in the lead. As preview audiences were less than enthusiastic about the film, MGM borrowed Laurel and Hardy from Hal Roach to add a few funny scenes. Unfortunately the film is believed to be lost. Laurel and Hardy's own first and, at the same time, best excursion in the filming of opera was „The Devil's Brother", a parody of Auber's comic opera „Fra Diavolo". The film is set in 18th century Italy. Stanlio and Ollio are made to help the gallant bandit Fra Diavolo move his booty and naturally ruin the whole plan for him. The high spots in the film are (alongside the funniest of all their scenes), Stan's grotesque physical absurdities: „fingerwiggle" and the complex „earsy, nosey, kneesy" game which drove Ollie as well as many viewers to despair in trying to copy it.

In Victor Herbert's (literally) fairy-tale-like film version of the operetta „Babes in Toyland" Stan and Ollie are workers in a toy factory who end up saving Toyland from the villain Barnaby. Since Santa Claus also plays a part here, the film is shown every year around Christmas on American television.

Their third film version of an opera, „The Bohemian Girl", is set, as the title suggests, in 18th century Bohemia. Stan and Ollie play travelling gypsies who discover a baby in their cart, which they then movingly look after. At the end of the film, it turns out that the girl is the daughter of a rich count, who he believed was dead. But the film has everything but a happy ending. Instead there is a ludicrous scene, typical for Laurel and Hardy: Ollie is stretched by two metres on the rack, while Stan is squashed to the size of a dwarf.

The operatic film „Swiss Miss" was the final and worst of Laurel and Hardy's musical trips. Here we see them as mousetrap-salesmen on the road in Switzerland who get into deep water and are sent to work in an Alpine hotel. In total, it may be said that the operatic films have an added attraction due to the pretty costumes and stunning sets and that they offer an original alternative to the other Laurel and Hardy films. Due to the long musical interludes sung by other people (in the four films, Stan and Ollie unfortunately sing only twice themselves), the pieces - like many of their full-length films - are too full of subplot, meaning that, despite many really funny scenes, the overall comic effect often gets lost.

MG 2894
MGM

Seite 70
„The Rogue Song", 1930. Stan als
„Ali-Bek" und Ollie als „Murza-Bek"

Page 70
„The Rogue Song", 1930. Stan as
„Ali-Bek" and Ollie as „Murza-Bek"

Seiten 72-74
Laurel und Hardys gelungenste
Lachoper „The Devil's Brother", 1933

Pages 72-74
Laurel and Hardy's best laughopera
„The Devil's Brother", 1933

Seiten 75 und 76
„Babes in Toyland", 1934.
Der kleine Junge ist Spanky,
Star der „Kleinen Strolche"

Pages 75 and 76
„Babes in Toyland", 1934.
The little boy is Spanky
the Star from the „Our Gang"

Seite 77
„The Bohemian Girl", 1936
Szenenfoto (oben), Stan und Ollie
bei einer Drehpause (unten)

Page 77
„The Bohemian Girl", 1936 filmstill (top),
Stan and Ollie during a shooting break
(bottom)

Seiten 78 und 79
„Swiss Miss", 1938. Stan und Ollie mit
der gebürtigen Österreicherin Della Lind

Pages 78 and 79
„Swiss Miss", 1938. Stan and Ollie with
Austrian born Della Lind

Stan und Ollie und die Frauen

Die Frauen nehmen sowohl in den Filmen von Laurel und Hardy als auch im Privatleben der beiden Komiker eine besondere Stellung ein. So waren Stan und Ollie nicht nur in ihren Filmen mit den unterschiedlichsten Frauen verheiratet, sondern auch in der Realität: Nach der Scheidung von seiner zweiten Ehefrau Myrtle heiratete Ollie am 7. März 1940 in Las Vegas Lucille Jones, die als Scriptgirl beim Laurel und Hardy-Film „The Flying Deuces" mitgearbeitet hatte.

Stan gestaltete sein Eheleben noch abwechslungsreicher: Mit der ersten Gattin, Lois, hatte er eine gemeinsame Tochter, bevor er sich im September 1935 für Virginia Ruth als zweite Gattin entschied. Schon bald darauf folgte die nächste Vermählung mit Vera Shuvalova. Doch auch diese Ehe verlief alles andere als harmonisch, und so kehrte Stan mit einer weiteren Heirat am 11. Januar 1941 zu Virginia Ruth zurück. Doch ähnlich wie Ollie sollte auch er erst mit seiner letzten Frau Ida Kiteva Raphael erfahren, was wahres Eheglück bedeutet. Dadurch, daß Laurel und Hardy ihre eigenen Namen auch im Film verwendeten, war es für die Presse jedesmal ein großes Vergnügen, die ehelichen Probleme der beiden Komiker jeweils mit großformatigen, ironischen Überschriften ans Licht der Öffentlichkeit zu zerren. Sicherlich waren Stans und Ollies private Probleme mit ein Grund dafür, daß vor allem die Gattinnen in ihren Filmen stets derart negativ dargestellt werden - wenn man auch keineswegs von einem Rachefeldzug der beiden Komiker gegen das „schwache Geschlecht" sprechen kann. Die Filmcharaktere Stan und Ollie sind vielmehr gar nicht in der Lage, eine normale Beziehung zu Frauen aufzubauen. Beide scheinen nämlich in ihrem eigenen Mikrokosmos zu leben, in den kein Dritter (und erst recht keine Frau) eintreten darf - andernfalls ist der Konflikt vorprogrammiert.

Sobald Stan und Ollie auf der Leinwand verheiratet sind, vermitteln die Ehen jeweils eher den Eindruck einer Mutter-Kind-Beziehung, in der die einzelnen Partnerinnen stets dominieren. Dabei entpuppen sich die Damen der Schöpfung oft sogar als regelrechte Hausdrachen, die Stan und Ollie nicht nur böse Worte, sondern auch massenweise Geschirr an den Kopf werfen (so in „Sons of the Desert"), auf ihre Gatten schießen („Be Big") und auch schon mal mit spitzer Axt hinter ihnen herjagen („Chickens Come Home"). Kein Wunder also, daß die beiden wiederholt versuchen, sich von ihren Frauen loszureißen. Doch selbst wenn ihnen dies im Einzelfall gelingt, geraten sie dann postwendend wieder an andere Frauen, die ihnen das Leben mindestens ebenso schwer machen wie ihre Gattinnen zu Hause ... Im Film „The Private Life of Oliver the Eighth" findet die Darstellung dieses Frauenbildes einen grausigen Höhepunkt: Eine Witwe, dargestellt von Mae Busch, will - nachdem sie zuvor eine Heiratsanzeige aufgegeben hat - Ollie als ihrem potentiellen nächsten Ehemann mit einem langen Messer die Kehle durchschneiden!

Stan and Ollie and women

Women play an important part for Laurel and Hardy both in their films as well as in their private lives. It was not just that Stan and Ollie were married to the most varied of women on screen, but in real life too. After his divorce from his second wife, Myrtle, on 7 March 1940 Ollie married Lucille Jones, the script girl who had worked on the Laurel and Hardy film „The Flying Deuces".

Stan's married life was even more varied. He had a daughter by his first marriage to Lois before deciding on Virginia Ruth as his second wife in September 1935. Shortly after this, there followed the next marriage to Vera Shuvalova. But this too was to run far from smoothly and, on 11 January 1941, Stan remarried Virginia Ruth. But, like Ollie, he was only to experience a happy marriage with his last wife, Ida Kiteva Raphael. Since Laurel and Hardy used their real names for their films, the press enjoyed parading the duo's marital problems with large-type, ironic headlines. Without doubt Stan and Ollie's private problems were one of the reasons why wives are always portrayed so negatively in their films - even if there can be no talk of a revenge campaign on the part of the two comedians aimed at the „fair sex". The film characters of Stan and Ollie are simply not able to develop a normal relationship with women. Both appear to live in their own microcosm, in which no third party (least of all a woman) may enter - at least not without a battle.

As soon as Stan and Ollie are married on screen, the marriages take on the appearance more of a mother-son relationship, in which the individual women are always the dominant partners. Often, the women in the films even turn out to be real battleaxes, who not only bombard Stan and Ollie with harsh words but also with piles of crockery (e.g., in „Sons of the Desert"), or shoot at their spouses („Be Big") and even chase after them with a sharpened axe („Chickens Come Home"). So it comes as no surprise that the two repeatedly try to escape from their wives. But even when they occasionally succeed, they soon run into other women who make their lives at least as difficult as life at home... The portrayal of women reaches its gruesome climax in the film „The Private Life of Oliver the Eighth", where a widow - played by Mae Busch - tries to slit the throat of her potential new husband, Ollie, after finding him through the lonely hearts!

Ollies späte Solokariere

Ollie's late solo career

Ließ Hal Roach seinen Mitarbeitern bei den Dreharbeiten quasi freie Hand, so bewies er beim Feilschen um Verträge doch in der Regel Kalkül und Geschäftssinn. Dadurch, daß er mit Laurel und Hardy stets zeitlich versetzt auslaufende Verträge abschloß, band er immer einen von beiden an sein Studio, so daß Stan und Ollie nie als Paar bei Vertragsverhandlungen auftreten konnten. Ende 1938 war vor allem die schlechte Presse über Laurels Ehe und seine damaligen Alkoholprobleme für Roach Anlaß genug, eine Hälfte seines populären Duos aus den Roach-Studios hinauszuwerfen. Dies führte zu Ollies erstem, ungewolltem Solofilm seit Beginn seiner Partnerschaft mit Stan Laurel. Roach verpflichtete den zu Stummfilmzeiten sehr bekannten Harry Langdon, um zusammen mit Hardy für den Film „Zenobia" vor die Kamera zu treten. Sogleich mutmaßte die Presse, Roach wolle aus den beiden ein neues Comedy-Team machen. Doch im fertigen Film waren Langdon und Hardy letztlich nur in wenigen gemeinsamen Szenen zu sehen. Der Film „Zenobia" ist eine charmante Komödie, in der Ollie einen Arzt spielt, der auf Bitten Harry Langdons die Aufgabe übernimmt, einen kranken Elefanten zu heilen. Daraufhin ist der Dickhäuter Ollie derart dankbar, daß er diesem nicht mehr von der Seite weicht. Nachdem es so zu allerlei Komplikationen in Hardys Familie gekommen ist, wendet sich am Ende doch alles zum Guten. Trotz seines Charmes war der Film kein großer Publikumserfolg, da die Zuschauer eine Fortsetzung der bekannten Laurel und Hardy-Filme erwartet hatten. Harry Langdon war jedoch ein ganz anderer Komiker als Stan Laurel, und so zeigte sich schmerzlich, daß weder Laurel noch Hardy durch irgendeinen anderen Künstler zu ersetzen waren. Dies mußte schließlich auch Roach einsehen, so daß er sich mit Stan schließlich auf einen neuen Vertrag einigte, demzufolge Laurel und Hardy gegebenenfalls die Roach-Studios für andere Filmprojekte gemeinsam verlassen konnten.

So war für Ollies zweite Solo-Rolle seiner späten Filmkarriere (1949 in dem Film „The Fighting Kentuckian") keineswegs ein Streit innerhalb des Teams die Ursache, sondern Stans Diabetes, die Ollies Partner zum Pausieren zwang. Hardy hatte die Rolle, die ihm sein Golffreund John Wayne anbot, zunächst sogar abgelehnt, um nicht erneut Gerüchte um eine Trennung von Stan aufkommen zu lassen. Erst, als ihn Stan zur Annahme der Filmrolle drängte, wagte Ollie, die Rolle des lustigen Trappers Willy Payne zu übernehmen, der John Wayne bei seinen Abenteuern unterstützt.

Bei seinem dritten Solo-Auftritt schließlich handelte es sich um eine kurze Gastrolle als Besucher einer Pferderennbahn in Bing Crosbys und Frank Capras Film „Riding High". Indem er in allen drei Filmen eine Rolle übernahm, die mit seinem bekannten Ollie-Charakter nichts zu tun hatte, bewies er dem Publikum, über welch breitgefächerte schauspielerische Fähigkeiten er verfügte.

If Hal Roach gave his staff a free reign on the set, he usually proved to be a calculating businessman when it came to haggling over contracts. In signing contracts with Laurel and Hardy which always terminated independently of each other, he ensured one of the two was always committed to the studios, making it impossible for Stan and Ollie to appear as a pair when it came to negotiating contracts. At the end of 1938, bad press about Laurel's marriage and his drinking were reason enough for Roach to throw one half of the popular duo out of his studios. This led to Ollie's first involuntary solo film since the start of his partnership with Stan Laurel. Roach hired Harry Langdon, who was very famous during the silent-movie era, to appear with Hardy in the film „Zenobia". The press immediately speculated that Roach wanted to create a new comedy team using the two. But in the completed film, Langdon and Hardy only appear together in a few scenes. The film „Zenobia" is a delightful comedy, in which Ollie plays a doctor who complies with Langdon's request to cure a sick elephant. The animal is then so grateful that it refuses to leave Ollie's side. Following all sorts of complications with Hardy's family, the film ends happily. Despite its obvious charm, the film was not a great hit with audiences, as the viewers expected a continuation of the well-known Laurel and Hardy films. But Harry Langdon was not at all the same type of comedian as Stan Laurel. The painful truth was that neither Laurel nor Hardy could be replaced by some other artiste. Even Roach had to finally concede this and agreed to a new contract with Stan which also allowed Laurel and Hardy to leave the Roach studios together for other film projects, if necessary.

Thus Ollie's second solo role much later on his film career (in the 1949 film „The Fighting Kentuckian") was in no way due to a dispute between the two, but to Stan's diabetes, which forced Stan to take a break. At first, Hardy turned down the part offered him by his golfing friend, John Wayne, so as not to allow fresh rumours of a split from Stan. Only when Stan pushed him to take on the part did Ollie dare to play the role of the comic trapper Willy Payne, who helps John Wayne in his adventures.

His third solo role was the brief guest appearance as a horse-racing spectator in Bing Crosby's and Frank Capra's „Riding High". In each of the three films he took on a character far removed from that of his well-known Ollie, allowing him to prove his outstanding acting talents.

Seite 84
Stan mit Vera Shuvalova, seiner dritten
Ehefrau, Ende der 30er Jahre

Page 84
Stan with Vera Shuvalova, his third wife,
at the end of the thirties

Seite 85
Oben:
Ollie heiratet seine dritte Ehefrau Lucille
im März 1940
Unten:
Laurel und Hardy mit ihren letzten
Ehefrauen, Ida und Lucille, in den 50er
Jahren

Page 85
Top:
Ollie marries his third wife Lucille,
March 1940
Bottom:
Laurel and Hardy with their final wives,
Ida and Lucille, in the early fifties

Seite 86 und 88
Ollie alleine und mit Harry Langdon
in „Zenobia", 1938

Page 86 and 88
Ollie alone and with Harry Langdon
in „Zenobia", 1938

Seite 89
Ollie vergnügt sich beim Hufeisenwerfen
während einer Drehpause von „Zenobia"

Page 89
Ollie's having fun horseshoe throwing
during a break from „Zenobia"

Die „großen" Studios

Noch während der Dreharbeiten zu „Saps at sea", ihrem letzten Film für Hal Roach, gründeten Laurel und Hardy im Jahre 1940 mit ihrem Anwalt Ben Shipman die „Laurel and Hardy Feature Productions". Vor allem Stan hoffte, als sein eigener Produzent fortan unabhängig arbeiten und in totaler künstlerischer Freiheit bessere Filme herstellen zu können. Da die drei jedoch zunächst keine Geldgeber für eine eigene Produktion auftreiben konnten, schlossen sie im April 1941 einen Vertrag mit der Filmgesellschaft 20th Century Fox über die Herstellung von zunächst einem Spielfilm ab - mit der Option auf neun weitere Filme. Da es sich nicht um einen Exklusivvertrag handelte, stand es Stan und Ollie sogar frei, zusätzlich noch für andere Gesellschaften Filme zu drehen. Obwohl Stan beim Verfassen des Drehbuchs für diesen Film („Great Guns") ein Mitspracherecht eingeräumt worden war, hatte er letztlich doch keine Möglichkeiten, dies auch durchzusetzen. Anders als bei Hal Roach waren in den großen Studios nämlich die Aufgaben der an einer Filmproduktion Beteiligten klar definiert: Stan, als Schauspieler engagiert, hatte ausschließlich vor der Kamera präsent zu sein (und nicht, wie er es gewohnt war, auch dahinter). Das spontane Improvisieren am Drehort - einst Stärke der beiden - wurde durch das strenge Festhalten am detaillierten Drehbuch verhindert. Jede Szene wurde jetzt mehrmals geprobt.

Danach drehten Stan und Ollie mit „A Haunting We Will Go" zunächst noch einen weiteren Film für die Fox-Company, bevor sie durch ihren Wechsel zu MGM auf bessere Arbeitsbedingungen hofften. Doch auch hier wurden ihre Erwartungen enttäuscht. Die Verantwortlichen waren nicht mit dem bis dahin für Laurel und Hardy typischen Modus Operandi vertraut. Hinzu kam, daß das ursprünglich clowneske, weiße Make-up der beiden Komiker plötzlich durch gewöhnliche, braune Schminke ersetzt wurde, so daß Stan und Ollie bereits dadurch viel älter wirkten als gewohnt (wodurch wiederum vor allem Stans kindliches Verhalten stark an Glaubwürdigkeit verlor). Größtes Manko der Filme war jedoch das schmerzhafte Fehlen der so beliebten Mitspieler aus der Roach-Ära. So konnten Laurel und Hardy außer ihren Namen sowie ein paar lieblos variierten, alten Gags leider kaum etwas aus ihren besten Tagen in die Produktionen der großen Filmfirmen hinüberretten.

Obwohl sich Stan und Ollie der völlig veränderten Arbeitsweise in den großen Studios bewußt waren, drehten sie aus finanziellen Gründen zunächst noch drei weitere Filme für die Fox sowie einen für MGM, bevor sie 1945 mit der Fox-Produktion „The bullfighters" endgültig ihren letzten gemeinsamen Hollywood-Film vorlegten. Ihren Abschied von der Leinwand gaben sie schließlich 1951 mit der französisch-britisch-italienischen Coproduktion „Atoll K" in Europa. Diese Komödie geriet allerdings eher zu einem Trauerspiel, da vor allem Stan im Verlauf der chaotischen Dreharbeiten durch Krankheit stark geschwächt war. Nicht nur wahren Fans dürften beim Betrachten des fertigen Films die Tränen gekommen sein.

The „big" studios

Laurel and Hardy formed „Laurel and Hardy Feature Productions" together with their lawyer, Ben Shipman, in 1940, while still working on „Saps at Sea", their last film for Hal Roach. Above all, being his own producer, Stan hoped to be able to work independently and to make better films with complete artistic licence. However, as the three of them initially could not find a financial backer, they signed a contract with 20th Century Fox in April 1941 to make one feature to begin with - with the option of nine further films. Since this was not an exclusive contract, Stan and Ollie were still at liberty to make films for other companies. Although Stan was allowed a say in the script-writing for this film („Great Guns"), he hardly had a chance to insist upon this right. As opposed to the Hal Roach studios, the tasks for those working on a film in the large studios were clearly defined. Stan, hired as an actor, was to stand in front of the camera (and not behind it, as was his wont). Strict compliance to the detailed script put paid to improvisation on the set - once the two comics' great strength. Each scene was repeatedly rehearsed.

Then, with „A Haunting We Will Go", Stan and Ollie made another film for Fox before switching to MGM in the hope of better working conditions. But here, too, they were disillusioned. Those responsible were not au fait with the typical working methods which Laurel and Hardy had previously been used to at Roach's studios with its well-initiated production crews. In addition to this, their original white, clownish make-up was suddenly replaced by the normal brown greasepaint, making Stan and Ollie look much older than usual (which, above all, undermined Stan's childish behaviour). What was painfully lacking the most, however, were the old favourites from the Roach era. Thus, apart from their names and a few mechanically rehashed gags, Laurel and Hardy were unfortunately unable to put much of their best into the big studios' productions.

Although Stan and Ollie were fully aware of the completely different methods used in the big studios, for financial reasons they first made three more films for Fox as well as one for MGM before finally making their last Hollywood movie together in 1945 for Fox, „The Bullfighters". Their farewell to the screen came in Europe in 1951, with the Franco-British-Italian co-production, „Robinson Crusoeland". Instead of being a comedy, this turned into a tragedy as, above all, Stan became considerably emaciated by illness during the chaotic shooting (with the result that not only true fans have to hold back the tears when watching the film).

Seite 90
Drehpause bei „Zenobia", Ollie
mit Adolphe Menjou **(oben)** sowie
Harry Langdon und Regisseur
Edward Sutherland **(unten rechts)**

Page 90
Shooting break at „Zenobia", Ollie
with Adolphe Menjou **(top)** and
with Harry Langdon and director
Edward Sutherland **(bottom right)**

Seite 91
Ollie mit John Wayne und
Vera Rawlston in
„The Fighting Kentuckian", 1949

Page 91
Ollie with John Wayne and Vera
Rawlston in „The Fighting Kentuckian",
1949

Seite 92
Stan und Ollie besprechen eine
Szene mit Regisseur Alfred Werker
während einer Drehpause von
„A-haunting we will go", 1942

Page 92
Stan and Ollie discuss a scene with
director Alfred Werker during a break
from „A-haunting we will go", 1942

Seite 94
Oben: „Jitterbugs", 1943
Unten: „Great Guns", 1941

Page 94
Top: „Jitterbugs", 1943
Bottom: „Great Guns", 1941

Seite 95
„The Dancing Masters", 1943

Page 95
„The Dancing Masters", 1943

Seiten 96 und 97
Stan als „Tante Emily" und Ollie in
„Jitterbugs"

Pages 96 and 97
Stan as „Aunt Emily" and Ollie in
„Jitterbugs"

Seiten 98 und 99
„The Big Noise", 1944

Pages 98 and 99
„The Big Noise", 1944

Seiten 100 und 101
Gagfotos von „A haunting we will go"

Pages 100 and 101
Gagshots from „A haunting we will go"

Von der Leinwand auf die Bühne

Im Jahre 1932 entschlossen sich Laurel und Hardy, gemeinsam einen Urlaub in England zu verbringen. Während Stan seine Verwandten besuchen wollte, plante Ollie, den berühmten britischen Golfplätzen einen Besuch abzustatten. Doch aus dem geplanten Urlaub wurde rasch eine (ungewollte) Publicity-Tour, derart euphorisch empfing man die beiden Komiker auf der Insel. Angesichts der Zuschauermassen während ihrer Ankunft wurde Stan und Ollie erstmals bewußt, wie berühmt sie wirklich waren.

Nachdem die beiden 1945 den großen Studios enttäuscht den Rücken gekehrt hatten und weitere Filmangebote zunächst ausblieben, bot ihnen Ende 1946 der englische Varieté-Besitzer Bernard Delfont an, eine sechswöchige Theatertournee durch das britische Königreich zu absolvieren. Damit war für Laurel und Hardy der erste Schritt für eine zweite, späte Karriere auf der Bühne vollzogen. Mit dem kurzen Stück „The Driver's Licence Sketch", welches Stan bereits 1940 geschrieben hatte, starteten sie am 24. Februar 1947 im „Empire" in Newcastle ihre Tournee durch Großbritannien. Der zwanzigminütige Sketch war in zwei Akte aufgeteilt und stellte, eingebettet in ein buntes Varieté-Programm, die Hauptattraktion des Abends dar. Kritiker und Publikum waren gleichermaßen begeistert, alle Vorstellungen ausverkauft. So traten Stan und Ollie allein in London sieben Wochen lang auf, bevor sie ihre umjubelte Bühnendarbietung fünf weitere Monate quer durch Großbritannien präsentierten. Im Oktober 1947 spielten sie in Dänemark sowie Schweden, fuhren dann mit dem Zug nach Paris, wo ein sechswöchiges Engagement im „Lido" auf sie wartete - auf der Fahrt dorthin kam es übrigens zu ihrem einzigen, sehr kurz geratenen Aufenthalt in Deutschland, als der verplombte Zug in Aachen auf ein anderes Gleis umgeleitet werden mußte. Im Anschluß an die Auftritte in Paris zogen sie mit ihrem Sketch eine weitere Woche durch Belgien, wo sie am 8. Januar 1948 ihre auf elf Monate ausgedehnte Reise in Gent beendeten. So erfolgreich sie auch in Europa waren, schien man sie in Hollywood seinerzeit vergessen zu haben. Dies wurde vor allem deutlich, als Stan 1949 krankheitsbedingt zu Hause bleiben mußte, während sich Ollie unter anderem mit John Wayne und Maureen O'Hara in dem Stück „What price glory?" erneut auf eine kurze Bühnentournee begab.

Im Jahre 1952, nachdem sich Laurel von den Strapazen während der Dreharbeiten zu „Atoll K" erholt hatte, absolvierten Laurel und Hardy erneut eine Theatertournee durch England. Diesmal präsentierten beide das von Stan verfaßte Stück „A Spot of Trouble", das stark an ihren gemeinsamen Film „Night owls" aus dem Jahre 1930 angelehnt war. Die siebenmonatige Tournee war wiederum sehr erfolgreich. Von Herbst 1953 bis Frühling 1954 schließlich begaben sich Stan und Ollie mit dem Stück „Birds of a feather", wiederum verfaßt von Stan Laurel, auf ihre endgültig letzte, jedoch nicht weniger erfolgreiche Theatertournee durch Großbritannien.

From screen to stage

In 1932, Laurel and Hardy decided to go on holiday together to England. While Stan intended to visit his relatives, Ollie wanted to see the famous British golf courses. But the holiday soon turned into an (unplanned) publicity tour, such was the warmth that greeted the two in England. It was only due to the crowds awaiting their arrival that the comic duo realised just how famous they were.

After Stan and Ollie had turned their backs in disappointment on the big studios in 1945, and no more film offers followed, at the end of 1946 the English music-hall owner Bernard Delfont offered them a six-week tour of theatres throughout the UK. This was the first step towards Laurel and Hardy's second and late (theatrical) career. On 24 February 1947 they started their British tour in the „Empire" in Newcastle, with the short play „The Driver's Licence Sketch", which Stan had written as early as 1940. The 20-minute sketch was split into two acts and was the highlight of the evening, incorporated in a mixed programme. Critics and audiences alike were impressed and it was a sell-out success. Consequently, Stan and Ollie appeared on stage for seven weeks in London alone, before touring the provinces for a further five months. In October 1947 they played in Denmark and Sweden, before going by train to Paris where they were booked for six weeks at the „Lido". (Incidentally, it was on the journey there that they paid their only, very brief visit to Germany as their sealed train had to be switched to another track in Aachen.) Following their appearances in Paris, they continued with their sketch for another week through Belgium, where they finished their journey in Ghent on 8 January 1948 (after performing in Antwerp, Brussels and Liège) - a tour which had stretched to eleven months. Although they may have been successful in Europe, they seemed to have been forgotten in Hollywood. This became manifestly obvious as Stan had to remain behind ill in 1949 while Ollie went on a short stage tour in „What Price Glory?", starring, among others, John Wayne and Maureen O'Hara.

In 1952, after Laurel had recovered from the exertion of working on „Robinson Crusoeland", Laurel and Hardy again toured the theatres of England. This time they presented Stan's play „A Spot of Trouble", which was heavily based on their 1930 film „Night Owls". The seven-month tour was also a success and even led the two comics to Ireland, where they appeared in Dublin and Belfast. Between the autumn of 1953 and spring 1954 Stan and Ollie went on their final - and just as successful - tour of Britain's theatres with the play „Birds of a Feather" (again written by Stan Laurel).

Magie
und Faszination

Magic
and fascination

Weder zuvor noch danach hat irgendein Komiker eine derart zeitlose wie universelle Ausstrahlung erreicht wie Stan Laurel und Oliver Hardy. Stan und Ollie sind auf der ganzen Welt bekannt, ihre Popularität ist auch sechzig Jahre nach der Hauptschaffensperiode der beiden Komiker ungebrochen. Bereits in ihrem Erscheinungsbild entsprechen die beiden dem Grundprinzip aller Komik, der Kontrastwirkung. Der dünne Stan scheint auf den ersten Blick der dümmere und dadurch komischere von beiden zu sein. Doch ist der dicke Ollie nicht etwa bloß der „ernste" Gegenpart, sondern ein unnachahmlicher, pompöser Besserwisser, der sich letzten Endes jedoch oft noch wesentlich ungeschickter anstellt als Stan - und damit mindestens genauso komisch wirkt. Dadurch, daß es in ihren Filmen keine klare Rollenverteilung zwischen ernst und komisch gibt, heben sich die beiden von anderen Komikerpaaren ab (die sich meist aus einem „Lustigen" und einem „Ernsten" zusammensetzten). Stan und Ollie gebärden sich wie Kinder, und das macht sie bei jung und alt gleichermaßen beliebt. Sie sind einerseits auf eine Art erwachsen, wie Kinder es gerne wären, andererseits aber auch hemmungslos kindisch, anarchistisch und albern, wie es sich mancher Erwachsene bisweilen für sich selbst erträumt.

Neben einzelnen komischen Standard-Verhaltensmustern, die jeder von beiden für sich entwickelt hat (Stans Kratzen am Kopf, seine Tränenausbrüche, Ollies mitleidheischende Blicke in die Kamera sowie sein verlegenes Wedeln mit der Krawatte), haben Laurel und Hardy vor allem zwei Methoden der Komik kreiert und bis zur Perfektion entwickelt: den „Slow burn" als das genaue Gegenteil der unüberlegten, schnellen Slapstick-Konfrontationen anderer Komiker sowie das „Tit for tat" - einen Schlagabtausch, den die Beteiligten jeweils mit einer geradezu pathetischen Ruhe und Gelassenheit vollziehen, so daß das Geschehen auf der Leinwand eher einer Ballettaufführung denn einer Schlacht ähnelt. Dabei läßt eine der Parteien ihrem Gegenüber jeweils ausreichend Zeit, sich in Ruhe die nächste Attacke zu überlegen, wobei ein jeder die einzelnen Angriffe seelenruhig über sich ergehen läßt, bevor er um so heftiger zurückschlägt, bis der Streit schließlich völlig eskaliert, Haus und Auto zerstört sind oder die Kleidung zerrissen ist.

Wenn sich Stan und Ollie streiten, einfach nur dumm anstellen oder etwas zerstören, dann tun sie dies mit einer derart souveränen Eleganz, daß sie und ihr Treiben (so übertrieben und unrealistisch es auch manchmal aussehen mag) für den Betrachter doch immer glaubwürdig bleibt. Laurel und Hardy wollen weder Mitleid erwecken, noch irgendeinen inhaltsschweren Appell an die Zuschauer richten; einzige Intention ihres Handelns ist es, den Betrachter zum Lachen zu bringen - und dies tun sie mit einer solch majestätischen Würde, daß sie völlig zu Recht als „Könige des Lachens" bezeichnet werden dürfen.

Never before nor after have any other comedians exuded the same kind of universal and timeless charisma as Stan Laurel and Oliver Hardy. Stan and Ollie are known worldwide and their popularity still has not dwindled sixty years after the high point of their creative period. In their appearance alone, the two adhere to that fundamental principle of comedy: a contrasting effect. Thin Stan appears at first the more foolish and thus funnier of the duo. But fat Ollie is not simply the „serious" counterpart, but is an inimitable, pompous know-all, who usually ends up making more of a fool of himself than Stan - and thus appears at least as comical. Since there is no clear distinction in their films as to who is serious and who comic, the pair stand out from other comedy duos (who are usually made up of the „funny one" and the „serious one"). Stan and Ollie behave like children and so are loved by young and old alike.

On the one hand they are adult in their own way, as children would like to be, but, on the other hand, are blatantly childish, anarchistic and ridiculous, like many adults wish they could be. Alongside individual comic standard characteristics, which each of them developed for himself (Stan's scratching his head, breaking out in tears, Ollie's long-suffering look at the camera and his embarrassed twiddling with his tie), Laurel and Hardy created, above all, two comic techniques which they then developed to perfection: the slow burn and the tit-for-tat. The first is the exact opposite of the spontaneous slapstick confrontations, found with other comics, and the other is an exchange of blows which the participants carry out with such an altogether pathetic coolness and calm, that the action on screen appears more like a ballet than a fight. Here, one of the two allows his opponent enough time to think of his next attack in peace, whereby each one allows himself to be attacked in all tranquillity before retaliating all the harder. Until the fight finally escalates out of all proportion and both house and car are destroyed or their clothes are completely ripped.

When Stan and Ollie fight, simply behave stupidly or destroy something, they do it with such supreme elegance that they and their actions (however exaggerated and unrealistic they may sometimes appear) still remain plausible in the viewers' eyes. Laurel and Hardy do not want to arouse sympathy nor do they want to make some heavily-laden appeal to the audience. Their only intention is to make the viewer laugh and they do this with such majestic dignity that they fully deserve the title of the „Kings of Comedy".

MGMP-6186

MCMP-6224

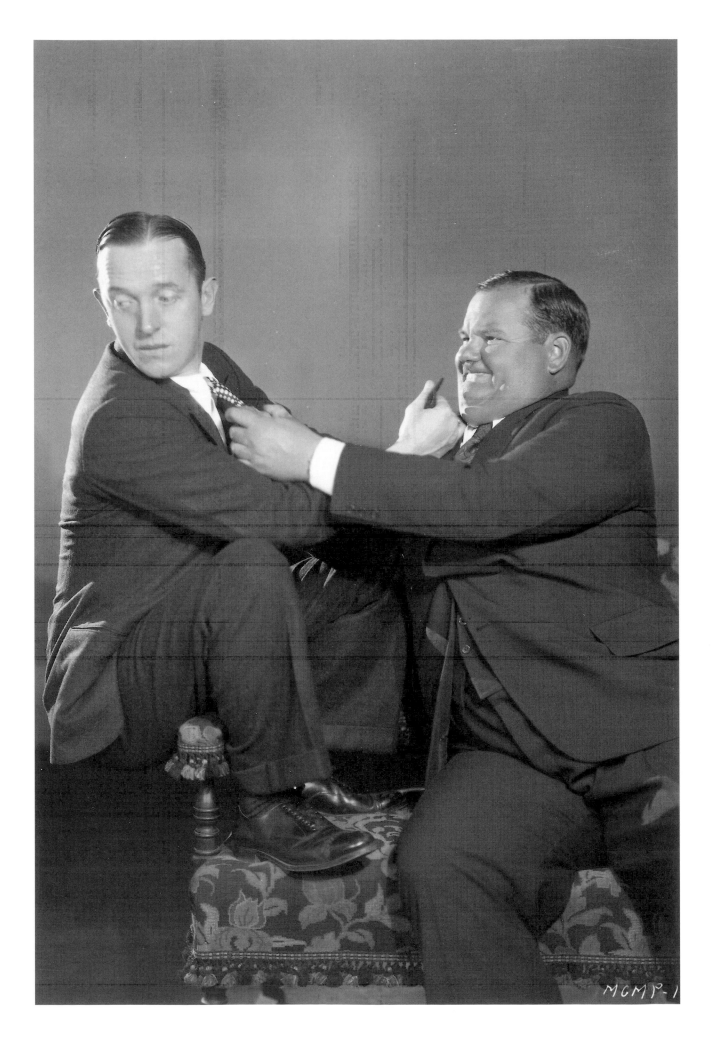

Sons of the Desert

Seit Mitte der sechziger Jahre existiert eine internationale Vereinigung von Laurel und Hardy-Liebhabern, die sich nach dem Film „Sons of the desert" („Die Wüstensöhne") benannt hat. Zu den Gründungsvätern zählte neben Stan Laurel auch der bekannte Laurel und Hardy-Biograph John McCabe. Eine Ulk-Verfassung, die Stan selbst mitausgearbeitet hat, garantiert, daß es auf den einzelnen Treffen der „Sons of the desert" nicht allzu ernst zugeht. Inzwischen hat sich der ursprünglich kleine Club zu einer großen, weltweiten Organisation entwickelt, deren Mitglieder - je nach Lust und Laune - Filmshows veranstalten, Stan und Ollie-Devotionalien austauschen und auch Clubzeitungen gestalten. Insgesamt zählt die Laurel und Hardy-Fangemeinde weltweit mehrere tausend Anhänger, die sich in mittlerweile über 200 „Tents" („Zelten") zusammengeschlossen haben. Nähere Informationen sind beim Verfasser dieses Buches erhältlich.

Since the mid-60s there has been an international association of Laurel and Hardy fans, named after the film „Sons of the Desert". Alongside Stan Laurel, one of the founding fathers was the Laurel and Hardy biographer, John McCabe. A humorous constitution, which Stan helped to write, ensures that the individual meetings of the Sons of the Desert are not taken so seriously. In the meantime, this initially small club has grown into a large, worldwide organisation and the members show films, swap Stan and Ollie memorabilia and even put together newsletters - as the mood takes them. In total, the Laurel and Hardy fan club has several thousand members around the globe, who have grouped together in over 200 „tents". Further information may be obtained from the author.

Harry Hoppe
Herderstraße 3
D-40237 Düsseldorf
harry@slowburn.de
www.slowburn.de

Filmografie

Filmography

Am Ende seines Lebens erfuhr Stan Laurel, der Hardy um sieben Jahre überlebte, späte Anerkennung in Hollywood. So wurde ihm am 17. April 1961 ein „Ehren-Oscar" für seine Pionierarbeit auf dem Gebiet der Filmkomik verliehen. Außerdem überreichten ihm Dana Andrews und Charlton Heston Ende 1964 mit dem „Screen Directors Guild Award" eine weitere Trophäe.

Das Vermächtnis von Laurel und Hardy besteht in ihren 106 gemeinsamen Filme, mit denen sie als der Welt größtes Komikerduo unsterblich wurden. Da eine entsprechende Liste in keinem Laurel und Hardy-Buch fehlen darf, sind die Filme im folgenden mit ihren wichtigsten Daten aufgeführt. Dabei beschränkt sich die Aufzählung auf die englischen Originaltitel.

At the end of his life, Stan Laurel, who outlived Hardy by seven years, was finally recognised by Hollywood. On 17 April 1961, he was awarded a special Oscar for creative pioneering in the field of cinema comedy. Furthermore, at the end of 1964, Dana Andrews and Charlton Heston presented him with another prize, the „Screen Directors Guild Award".

Laurel and Hardy's legacy is a total of 106 films together, which will ensure they remain immortal comics until the end of time. Since no Laurel and Hardy book is complete without such a list, here are the films with the essential data.

Min. = Minuten
P   = Produzent
R/D = Regisseur
S/A = wichtigste Schauspieler neben
       Laurel und Hardy
*   = Gastauftritt

Min. = Minutes
P   = Producer
R/D = Director
S/A = Main Actors beneath
       Laurel and Hardy
*   = Guest appearance

1918

THE LUCKY DOG
ca. 20 Min.
P: Gilbert M. Anderson
R/D: Jess Robbins
S/A: Florence Gillet

1926

45 MINUTES FROM HOLLYWOOD
ca. 20 Min.
P: Hal Roach
R/D: Fred L. Guiol
S/A: Glen Tyron, Theda Bara, Our Gang

1927

DUCK SOUP
ca. 20 Min.
P: Hal Roach
R/D: Fred L. Guiol
S/A: Madeleine Herlock, William Austin

SLIPPING WIVES
ca. 20 Min.
P: Hal Roach
R/D: Fred L. Guiol
S/A: Priscilla Dean, Albert Conti

LOVE 'EM AND WEEP
ca. 20 Min.
P: Hal Roach
R/D: Fred L. Guiol
S/A: Mae Busch, James Finlayson

WHY GIRLS LOVE SAILORS
ca. 20 Min.
P: Hal Roach
R/D: Fred L. Guiol
S/A: Viola Richard, Anita Garvin

WITH LOVE AND HISSES
ca. 20 Min.
P: Hal Roach
R/D: Fred L. Guiol
S/A: James Finlayson, Anita Garvin

SAILORS, BEWARE!
ca. 20 Min.
P: Hal Roach
R/D: Hal Yates
S/A: Anita Garvin, Stanley Sandford

NOW I'LL TELL ONE
ca. 20 Min.
P: Hal Roach
R/D: James Parrott
S/A: Charley Chase, Edna Marion

DO DETECTIVES THINK?
ca. 20 Min.
P: Hal Roach
R/D: Fred L. Guiol
S/A: James Finlayson, Viola Richard

SUGAR DADDIES
ca. 20 Min.
P: Hal Roach
R/D: Fred L. Guiol
S/A: James Finlayson, Noah Young

THE SECOND HUNDRED YEARS
ca. 20 Min.
P: Hal Roach
R/D: Fred L. Guiol
S/A: James Finlayson, Stanley Sandford

CALL OF THE CUCKOOS *
ca. 20 Min.
P: Hal Roach
R/D: Clyde Bruckman
S/A: Max Davidson, Charley Chase

HATS OFF
ca. 20 Min.
P: Hal Roach
R/D: Hal Yates
S/A: James Finlayson, Anita Garvin

PUTTING PANTS ON PHILLIP
ca. 20 Min.
P: Hal Roach
R/D: Clyde Bruckman
S/A: Sam Lufkin, Harvey Clarke

THE BATTLE OF THE CENTURY
ca. 20 Min.
P: Hal Roach
R/D: Clyde Bruckman
S/A: Charlie Hall, Anita Garvin

1928

LEAVE 'EM LAUGHING
ca. 20 Min.
P: Hal Roach
R/D: Clyde Bruckman
S/A: Edgar Kennedy, Charlie Hall

FLYING ELEPHANTS
ca. 20 Min.
P: Hal Roach
R/D: Fred Butler
S/A: James Finlayson, Dorothy Coburn

THE FINISHING TOUCH
ca. 20 Min.
P: Hal Roach
R/D: Clyde Bruckman
S/A: Edgar Kennedy, Dorothy Coburn

FROM SOUP TO NUTS
ca. 20 Min.
P: Hal Roach
R/D: Edgar Kennedy
S/A: Anita Garvin, Stanley Sandford

YOU'RE DARN' TOOTIN'
ca. 20 Min.
P: Hal Roach
R/D: Edgar Kennedy
S/A: Sam Lufkin, Rolfe Sedan

THEIR PURPLE MOMENT
ca. 20 Min.
P: Hal Roach
R/D: James Parrott
S/A: Anita Garvin, Jimmy Aubrey

SHOULD MARRIED MEN GO HOME?
ca. 20 Min.
P: Hal Roach
R/D: James Parrott
S/A: Edgar Kennedy, Viola Richard

EARLY TO BED
ca. 20 Min.
P: Hal Roach
R/D: Emmett Flynn

TWO TARS
ca. 20 Min.
P: Hal Roach
R/D: James Parrott
S/A: Thelma Hill, Ruby Blaine

HABEAS CORPUS
ca. 20 Min.
P: Hal Roach
R/D: James Parrott
S/A: Richard Carle, Charley Rogers

WE FAW DOWN
ca. 20 Min.
P: Hal Roach
R/D: Leo McCarey
S/A: Bess Flowers, Vivian Oakland

1929

LIBERTY
ca. 20 Min.
P: Hal Roach
R/D: Leo McCarey
S/A: James Finlayson, Jean Harlow

WRONG AGAIN
ca. 20 Min.
P: Hal Roach
R/D: Leo McCarey
S/A: Del Henderson, Charlie Hall

THAT'S MY WIFE
ca. 20 Min.
P: Hal Roach
R/D: Lloyd French
S/A: Vivian Oakland, Charlie Hall

BIG BUSINESS
ca. 20 Min.
P: Hal Roach
R/D: James Horne
S/A: James Finlayson, Stanley Sandford

UNACCUSTOMED AS WE ARE
ca. 20 Min.
P: Hal Roach
R/D: Lewis Foster
S/A: Edgar Kennedy, Thelma Todd

DOUBLE WHOOPEE
ca. 20 Min.
P: Hal Roach
R/D: Lewis Foster
S/A: John Peters, Jean Harlow

BERTH MARKS
ca. 20 Min.
P: Hal Roach
R/D: Lewis Foster
S/A: Harry Bernard, Charlie Hall

MEN 'O WAR
ca. 20 Min.
P: Hal Roach
R/D: Lewis Foster
S/A: James Finlayson, Harry Bernard

THE HOLLYWOOD REVUE OF 1929 *
1ca. 20 Min.
P: Harry Rapf
R/D: Charles F. Riesner
S/A: Jack Benny, Joan Crawford, John Gilbert

PERFECT DAY
ca. 20 Min.
P: Hal Roach
R/D: James Parrott
S/A: Edgar Kennedy, Key Deslys

THEY GO BOOM
ca. 20 Min.
P: Hal Roach
R/D: James Parrott
S/A: Charlie Hall, Sam Lufkin

BACON GRABBERS
ca. 20 Min.
P: Hal Roach
R/D: Lewis Foster
S/A: Edgar Kennedy, Jean Harlow

THE HOOSE GOW
ca. 20 Min.
P: Hal Roach
R/D: James Parrott
S/A: James Finlayson, Stanley Sandford

ANGORA LOVE
ca. 20 Min.
P: Hal Roach
R/D: Lewis Foster
S/A: Edgar Kennedy, Charlie Hall

1930

NIGHT OWLS
ca. 20 Min.
P: Hal Roach
R/D: James Parrott
S/A: James Finlayson, Edgar Kennedy

BLOTTO
ca. 30 Min.
P: Hal Roach
R/D: James Parrott
S/A: Anita Garvin, Charlie Hall

BRATS
ca. 20 Min.
P: Hal Roach
R/D: James Parrott

BELOW ZERO
ca. 20 Min.
P: Hal Roach
R/D: James Parrott
S/A: Charlie Hall, Frank Holliday

THE ROGUE SONG
115 Min.
P: Lionel Barrymore
R/D: Lionel Barrymore
S/A: Lawrence Tibbett
(In Farbe / In colour)

HOG WILD
ca. 20 Min.
P: Hal Roach
R/D: James Parrott
S/A: Fay Holderness, Doro Granger

THE LAUREL & HARDY MURDER CASE
ca. 30 Min.
P: Hal Roach
R/D: James Parrott
S/A: Stanley Sandford, Fred Kesley

ANOTHER FINE MESS
ca. 30 Min.
P: Hal Roach
R/D: James Parrott
S/A: James Finlayson, Thelma Todd

1931

BE BIG
ca. 30 Min.
P: Hal Roach
R/D: James Parrott
S/A: Anita Garvin, Isa Keith

CHICKENS COME HOME
ca. 30 Min.
P: Hal Roach
R/D: James Horne
S/A: James Finlayson, Mae Busch, Thelma Todd

THE STOLEN JOOLS
ca. 20 Min.
P: Pat Casey
R/D: Willian McGann
S/A: Buster Keaton, Our Gang

LAUGHING GRAVY
ca. 30 Min.
P: Hal Roach.
R/D: James Horne
S/A: Charlie Hall, Harry Bernard

OUR WIFE
ca. 20 Min.
P: Hal Roach
R/D: James Horne
S/A: James Finlayson, Babe London, Ben Turpin

PARDON US
56 Min.
P: Hal Roach
R/D James Parrott
S/A: James Finlayson, Walter Long

COME CLEAN
ca. 20 Min.
P: Hal Roach
R/D: James Horne
S/A: Mae Busch, Charlie Hall

ONE GOOD TURN
ca. 20 Min.
P: Hal Roach
R/D: James Horne
S/A: James Finlayson, Mary Carr, Bill Gilbert

BEAU HUNKS
40 Min.
P: Hal Roach
R/D: James Horne
S/A: Charles Middleton

ON THE LOOSE *
ca. 20 Min.
P: Hal Roach.
R/D: Hal Roach.
S/A: Thelma Todd, Zasu Pitts

1932

HELPMATES
ca. 20 Min.
P: Hal Roach
R/D: James Parrott
S/A. Blanche Payson, Bobby Burns

ANY OLD PORT
ca. 20 Min.
P: Hal Roach
R/D: James Parrott
S/A: Walter Long, Julie Bishop

THE MUSIC BOX
ca. 20 Min.
P: Hal Roach
R/D: James Parrott
S/A: Billy Gilbert, Charlie Hall

THE CHIMP
ca. 30 Min.
P: Hal Roach
R/D: James Parrott
S/A: James Finlayson, Billy Gilbert

COUNTY HOSPITAL
ca. 20 Min.
P: Hal Roach
R/D: James Parrott
S/A: Billy Gilbert, Sam Lufkin

SCRAM!
ca. 20 Min.
P: Hal Roach
R/D: Ray McCarey
S/A: Rychard Cramer, Sam Lufkin

PACK UP YOUR TROUBLES
68 Min.
P: Hal Roach
R/D: George Marshall
S/A: James Finlayson, Charles Middleton

THEIR FIRST MISTAKE
ca. 20 Min.
P: Hal Roach
R/D: George Marshall
S/A: Mae Busch, Billy Gilbert

TOWED IN A HOLE
ca. 20 Min.
P: Hal Roach
R/D: George Marshall
S/A: Billy Gilbert

1933

TWICE TWO
ca. 20 Min.
P: Hal Roach
R/D: James Parrott
S/A: Charlie Hall, Baldwin Cooke

ME AND MY PAL
ca. 20 Min.
P: Hal Roach
R/D: Charles Rodgers
S/A: James Finlayson, Eddie Dunn

THE DEVIL'S BROTHER
90 Min.
P: Hal Roach
R/D: Hal Roach
S/A: James Finlayson, Thelma Todd

THE MIDNIGHT PATROL
ca. 20 Min.
P: Hal Roach
R/D: Lloyd French
S/A: Robert Kortman, Charlie Hall

BUSY BODIES
ca. 20 Min.
P: Hal Roach
R/D: Lloyd French
S/A: Charlie Hall, Stan Sandford

WILD POSES *
ca. 20 Min.
P: Robert McGowan
R/D: Robert McGowan
S/A: Our Gang

DIRTY WORK
ca. 20 Min.
P: Hal Roach
R/D: Lloyd French
S/A: Lucien Littlefield

SONS OF THE DESERT
68 Min.
P: Hal Roach
R/D: William Seiter
S/A: Mae Busch, Charley Chase

1934

THE PRIVATE LIFE OF OLIVER THE EIGHTH
ca. 30 Min.
P: Hal Roach
R/D: Lloyd French
S/A: Mae Busch, Jack Beaty

HOLLYWOOD PARTY *
68 Min.
P: Harry Rapf
R/D Allen Dawn
S/A: Lupe Velez, Jimmy Durante

GOING BYE-BYE
ca. 20 Min.
P: Hal Roach
R/D: Charles Rogers
S/A: Walter Long, Mae Busch

THEM THAR HILLS
ca. 20 Min.
P: Hal Roach
R/D: Charles Rogers
S/A: Mae Busch, Charlie Hall

BABES IN TOYLAND
79 Min.
P: Hal Roach
R/D: Gus Meins
S/A: Felix Knight, Henry Brandon

THE LIVE GHOST
ca. 20 Min.
P: Hal Roach
R/D: Charles Rogers
S/A: Charlie Hall, Walter Long

1935

TIT FOR TAT
ca. 20 Min.
P: Hal Roach
R/D: Charles Rogers
S/A: Mae Busch, Charlie Hall

THE FIXER UPPERS
ca. 20 Min.
P: Hal Roach
R/D: Charles Rogers
S/A: Charles Middleton, Mae Busch

THICKER THAN WATER
ca. 20 Min.
P: Hal Roach
R/D: James Horne
S/A: James Finlayson, Daphne Pollard

BONNIE SCOTLAND
80 Min.
P: Hal Roach
R/D: James Horne
S/A: James Finlayson, June Lang

1936

THE BOHEMIAN GIRL
70 Min
P: Hal Roach
R/D: James Horne
S/A: Antonio Moreno, Mae Busch

ON THE WRONG TRECK *
ca. 20 Min.
P: Hal Roach
R/D: Charley Chase
S/A. Charley Chase

OUR RELATIONS
74 Min.
P: Hal Roach
R/D: Harry Lachman
S/A: James Finlayson, Daphne Pollard

1937

WAY OUT WEST
65 Min.
P: Hal Roach
R/D: James Horne
S/A: James Finlayson, Rosina Lawrence

PICK A STAR *
70 Min.
P: Hal Roach
R/D: Edward Sedgewick
S/A: Patsy Kelly, James Finlayson, Jack Haley

1938

SWISS MISS
72 Min.
P: Hal Roach
R/D: John Blystone
S/A: Della Lind, Anita Garvin

BLOCKHEADS
58 Min.
P: Hal Roach
R/D: John Blystone
S/A: James Finlayson, Billy Gilbert

1939

THE FLYING DEUCES
69 Min.
P: Boris Morros
R/D: Edward Sutherland
S/A: James Finlayson, Charles Middleton

1940

A CHUMP AT OXFORD
63 Min.
P: Hal Roach
R/D: Alfred Goulding
S/A: Wilfred Lucas, Frank Baker

SAPS AT SEA
57 Min.
P: Hal Roach
R/D: Gordon Douglas
S/A: James Finlayson, Ben Turpin, Rychard

1941

GREAT GUNS
74 Min.
P: Sol Wurtzel
R/D: Monty Banks
S/A: Sheila Ryan, Dick Nelson

1942

A-HAUNTING WE WILL GO
67 Min.
P: Sol Wurtzel
R/D: Alfred Werker
S/A: Sheila Ryan, Dante

1943

THE TREE IN A TEST TUBE
10 Min.
P: Department of Agriculture
R/D: Charles McDonald
(In Farbe / In colour)

AIR RAID WARDENS
67 Min.
P: B. Zeidman
R/D: Edward Sedgewick
S/A: Edgar Kennedy, Jaqueline White

JITTERBUGS
74 Min.
P: Sol Wurtzel
R/D: Mal St.Clair
S/A: Vivian Blaine, Robert Bailey

THE DANCING MASTERS
63 Min.
P: Lee Marcus
R/D: Mal St. Clair
S/A: Trudy Marshall, Robert Mitchum

1944

THE BIG NOISE
74 Min.
P: Sol Wurtzel
R/D: Mal St. Clair
S/A: Doris Merrick, Athur Space

1945

NOTHING BUT TROUBLE
70 Min.
P: B. Zeidman
R/D: Sam Taylor
S/A: Mary Bolard, Henry O'Neill

THE BULLFIGHTERS
69 Min.
P: William Girard
R/D: Mal St. Clair
S/A: Margo Woode, Richard Lane

1951

ATOLL K
98 Min.
P: Raymond Eger
R/D: Leo Joannon
S/A: Suzy Delair, Max Elloy

Laurel und Hardy in Farbe

Laurel and Hardy in color

Die Filme von Laurel und Hardy wurden alle in Schwarz/Weiss gedreht. Einzige Ausnahme ist ihr Gastauftritt in der Opernverfilmung „The Rouge Song" von 1929 (siehe Seite 70). Der Film gilt in seiner Gesamtheit leider als verschollen. Es existierte jahrelang lediglich eine Szene. In dieser sind Laurel und Hardy jedoch nur schlecht zu erkennen, da sie vor einem Sturm in eine dunkle Höhle flüchten. Mitte der Neunziger Jahre hat man im Prager Filmmuseum eine zehnminütige Rolle mit einigen Gesangsszenen, leider ohne die beiden Komiker, entdeckt. Einen weiteren „farbigen" Auftritt hatten die beiden im Auftrag des US-Landwirtschaftsministeriums: „The Tree in a test Tube" wurde 1943 in Kodachrome gedreht. Laurel und Hardy werden darin von einem nur aus dem „Off" zu hörenden Sprecher belehrt, welche von ihnen mitgeführten Alltagsgegenstände aus Holzmaterialien bestehen. Man erkennt Laurels rotes Haar und Hardys braungebranntes Gesicht. Im Privatbesitz existieren darüber hinaus noch farbige Szenen von einem Theaterauftritt, von einem gemeinsamen Beisammensein im Garten (aufgenommen kurz vor Hardys Tod, Stan macht hier einen recht abgemagerten Eindruck) sowie mit dem alternden Stan Laurel am Schreibtisch, der mit zwei L&H Marionetten spielt. Nach wie vor hält sich auch das Gerücht, daß der Spielfilm „Swiss Miss" von 1938 komplett in Technicolor gedreht worden sein soll, aus Geldmangel jedoch nur auf Schwarz/Weiss-Material kopiert wurde.

Anfang der achtziger Jahre wurden erstmalig Laurel und Hardy-Filme koloriert. War die Qualität der ersten eingefärbten Kurzfilme noch eher dürftig, wurde das Verfahren im Laufe der Zeit immer mehr perfektioniert. So geriet die farbige Videofassung von „Way out West" 1985 in Amerika zu einem Riesenerfolg. Stan Laurel erzählte dem Biografen John McCabe, er habe es immer bedauert, daß der Film „Babes in Toyland" aufgrund seines farbigen Spielzeugland-Dekors nicht in Farbe gedreht wurde. Bei aller berechtigten Kritik über die Verfremdung mancher Filme anderer Genres durch die Kolorierung ist die farbige Fassung von „Babes in Toyland" einfach wundervoll.

Zur Abrundung dieses Kapitels sind auf den nächsten Seiten Kinoplakate mit Laurel und Hardy sowie weitere farbige Werbematerialien aus aller Welt abgebildet.

All the Laurel and Hardy movies were shot in black and white. The only exception here being their 1929 cameo appearance in the opera "The Rogue Song" (cf. page 70). However, no single copy of the entire film is known to exist. For years just the one scene existed, but Laurel and Hardy are hardly recognizable in this as they seek shelter from a storm in a dark cave. Sometime in the mid-90s a 10-minute reel was discovered at the Prague film museum, containing some songs, but unfortunately not featuring our two heroes. Laurel and Hardy did have another "colorful" appearance thanks to the US Department of Agriculture. The 1943 "The Tree in a test Tube" was shot in Kodachrome and we see the two comics being told by a voice off which of their everyday objects is made of wood. Stanley's red hair is recognizable as is Ollie's sun-tanned face. There are also some privately owned color films of one of their theater appearances, of a get-together in the garden (shortly before Hardy's death with Laurel looking very thin) as well as one of Stan sitting at a desk playing with two Laurel and Hardy puppets. And there is still the rumor that the 1938 feature "Swiss Miss" was shot entirely in Technicolor but only printed in black and white to save money.

The beginning of the 80s saw the first coloring of Laurel and Hardy movies. While this process was very poor at the start, the technique was perfected over time, such that the colored video version of "Way out West" was a huge success when it was released in America in 1985. Stan Laurel told his biographer, John McCabe, that he always regretted the fact that "Babes in Toyland", with its colorful scenery, was not shot in color. Despite the justified criticism leveled at this "disfiguring" of movies belonging to other genres, the color version of "Babes in Toyland" is a sheer delight.

We would like to round off this chapter with some movie theater posters featuring Laurel and Hardy as well as other colorful promotional material from around the world.

Amerikanisches Filmplakat zu Laurel und Hardys erstem gemeinsamen Film, ca. 1921
American movie poster for Laurel and Hardy's first film appearence, ca. 1921

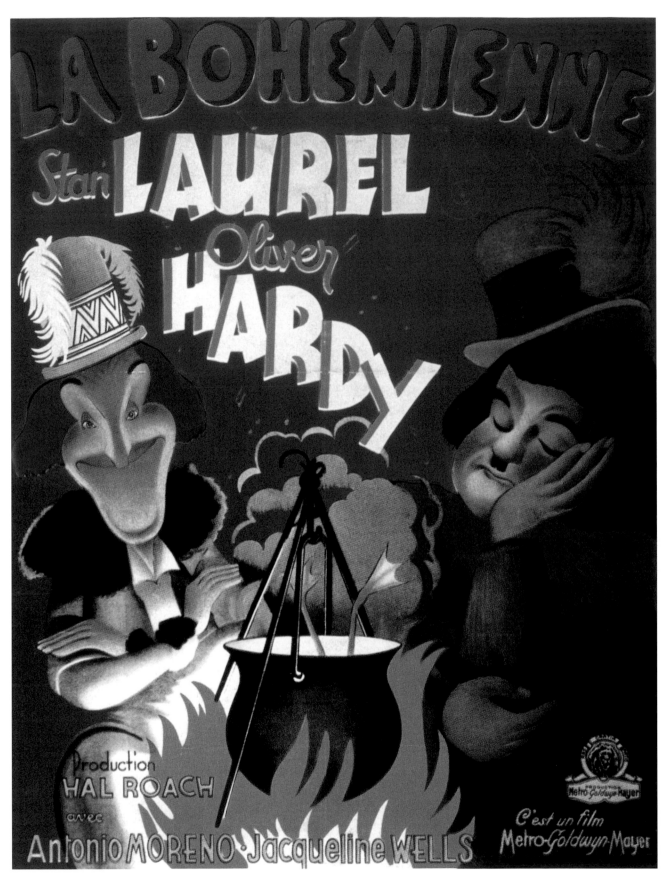

Französisches Filmplakat zu „The Bohemian Girl", 1936
French movie poster for "The Bohemian Girl", 1936

Holländisches Filmplakat, 1933
Dutch movie poster, 1933

Amerikanische Titelkarte, 1934
American title card, 1934

Amerikanische Titelkarte, 1934
American title card, 1934

Amerikanisches Filmplakat, 1933
American one sheet poster, 1933

Laurel und Hardy in Farbe
Laurel and Hardy in color

Spanisches Filmplakat zu „Way Out West", 1937
Spanish movie poster for "Way Out West", 1937

Amerikanische Titelkarte, 1941
American title card, 1941

Amerikanische Titelkarte, 1932
American title card, 1932

Dänisches Filmplakat zu „Pardon Us", 1962
Danish movie poster for "Pardon Us", 1962

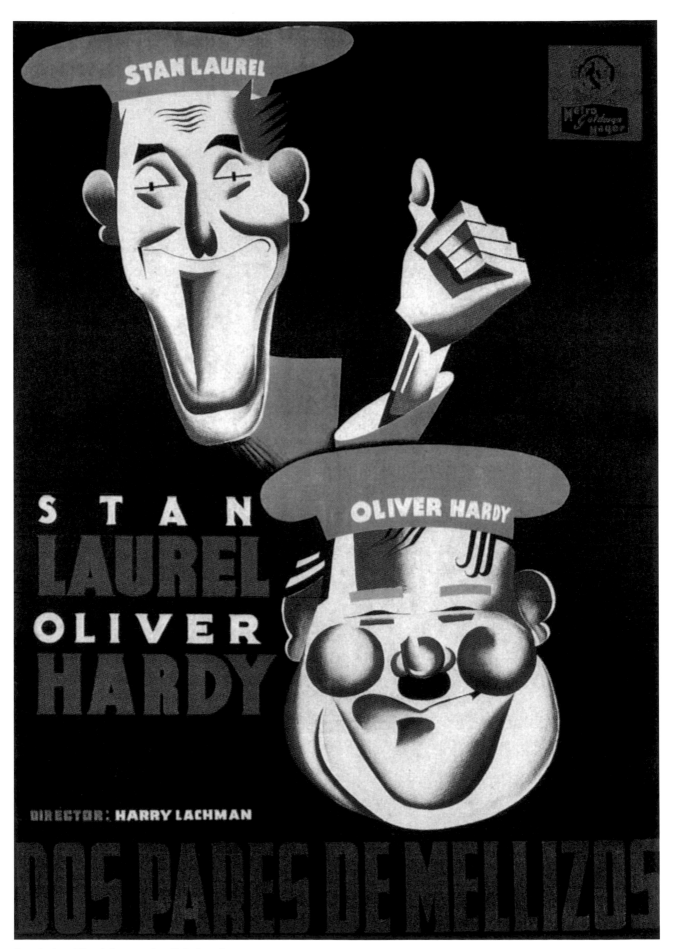

Spanisches Filmplakat zu „Our Relations", 1936
Spanish movie poster for "Our Relations", 1936

Amerikanische Titelkarte, 1944
American title card, 1944

Amerikanische Titelkarte, 1937
American title card, 1937

Spanisches Filmplakat zu „A Chump at Oxford", 1965
Spanish movie poster for "A Chump at Oxford", 1965

Deutsches Filmplakat zu „Atoll K", 1954
German movie poster for "Atoll K", 1954

Italienisches Filmplakat zu „Swiss Miss",1963
Italian movie poster for "Swiss Miss", 1963